UNIQUE STORIES and FACTS from LDS HISTORY

MORMON
HISTORY
101

DAN BARKER

UNIQUE STORIES AND FACTS FROM LDS HISTORY

MORMON
HISTORY
101

DAN BARKER

CFI
Springville, Utah

This is not an official publication of The Church of Jesus Christ of Latter-day Saints. The opinions and views expressed herein belong solely to the author and do not necessarily represent the opinions or views of Cedar Fort, Inc. Permission for the use of sources, graphics, and photos is also solely the responsibility of the author.

Editor's Note: Spelling and grammar in quotes have been modernized. The acronym HBLL refers to the Harold B. Lee Library on the campus of Brigham Young University, which houses a special collection of original church history and pioneer documents.

ISBN 13: 978-1-59955-798-4

Published by CFI, an imprint of Cedar Fort, Inc., 2373 W. 700 S., Springville, UT 84663
Distributed by Cedar Fort, Inc., www.cedarfort.com

LIBRARY OF CONGRESS CATALOGING-IN-PUBLICATION DATA

Barker, Dan, 1958 – author.
  Mormon history 101 / Dan Barker.
    p. cm.
  Summary: Contains historical facts about the Mormon Church. Includes
trivia and multiple choice questions to test the reader's knowledge of
Mormon history.
  ISBN 978-1-59955-798-4
  1. Church of Jesus Christ of Latter-day Saints—History—19th century. 2.
Mormon Church—History—19th century. I. Title.

  BX8611.B3185 2011
  289.309—dc22

                          2011000396

Cover design by Angela D. Olsen
Cover design © 2011 by Lyle Mortimer
Edited and typeset by Heidi Doxey

Printed in the United States of America

10 9 8 7 6 5 4 3 2 1

Printed on acid-free paper

FOR MORE INSPIRING anecdotes and events from Church history, be sure to check out Dan Barker's *Unique Stories & Facts from LDS History.*

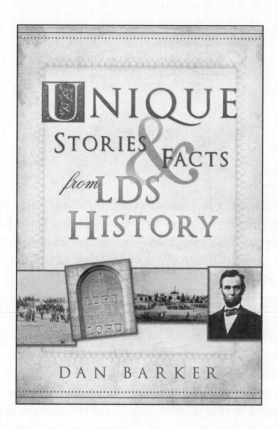

AS LATTER-DAY SAINTS, we are indeed a peculiar people with an extraordinary history. Increase your faith as you read the unbelievable, the never-before-heard, or the seldom-heard stories from Church history.

THESE STORIES MAY not be well-known, but each has contributed to the Latter-day Saints' one-of-a-kind history and culture. In this fascinating volume, Dan Barker has compiled hundreds of facts that entertain, inspire, and teach. *Unique Stories & Facts from LDS History* is sure to spice up a family home evening, liven up a talk, or apply finishing touches to a lesson.

ACKNOWLEDGMENTS

A sincere thank you goes out to my eldest son, James, for the suggestion. His idea to compile stacks of material into a book that all could enjoy, rather than just the youth I taught, got the wheels in motion for my first book, *Unique Stories & Facts from LDS History*, and that motion continues with *Mormon History 101*. Another thank you must go out to my wife, Kate. Never once did she complain as she saw her kitchen and dining area transformed into a temporary Library of Congress. I literally buried myself in stacks of material, eating up every square inch of available baking and dining space.

And finally, to the staff at Cedar Fort, particularly Jennifer Fielding, the editors, and the design team. It was Jennifer's suggestions that kept the fire burning in this amateur author, and the patience of the editors to work with me and my lack of command of the English language. I'm still in awe of the cover designs and the layout created by the design team. Thank you all!

CONTENTS

Introduction:
How Does This Book Work?

Every question deserves an answer, and every answer originates from a fact, or what I refer to as a fact story. Trust me, there is an innumerable supply of fact stories that relate to the Church. They serve to pique interest, answer inquiries, and strengthen testimonies. The Church of Jesus Christ of Latter-day Saints has a proud heritage and an equally compelling history. This legacy is arguably as loaded and complex as the legacy of any other group in the world.

We are blessed with a rich tradition, which can only create enthusiasm as one delves into the doctrines and journals of those who have preceded us. For instance, we are all familiar with the scenes associated with the establishment of the Church. We never weary at the story of the heavenly manifestation in a grove of trees just a stone's throw from the Smith cabin. The same could be said of the angel Moroni's visit to the young Joseph Smith. This is familiar territory because we have heard these stories on many occasions and appreciate them. We realize they are an integral part of the foundation to our testimonies.

The question might be asked, though, did the angel Moroni visit other individuals in the Church? Well, of course he did; we know this. We know that he visited the Three Witnesses, Mary Whitmer, and a few other Church members. The question then might be asked, did Moroni only influence people in his generation and the generation of the Prophet Joseph Smith? It's an intriguing thought, one that we most likely would dismiss as just that—intriguing, and nothing more. However, with a little more research, one might discover that Orson Hyde shed light on

1

this question when he revealed that the angel Moroni influenced two historical "celebrities" in two different centuries. Definitely captivating, fascinating, absorbing, stimulating, or whatever adjective you care to use.

The questions asked and answers revealed in this book are intended to do just this—stimulate, absorb, fascinate, or captivate through the corresponding fact or fact story. In my first book, *Unique Stories & Facts from LDS History*, I made it easy on you by providing you with these stories with very little work on your part; all you had to do was read. In *Mormon History 101*, I make you work a little harder. You will be asked a question with four multiple choice answers. Be brave, give it a try, and take the test. Then go to the end of the chapter, where the answer is given along with the story or fact that accompanies it. I even tossed in a few true or false questions to increase your chances at a better score.

Now, I realize that what may be new and exciting to one individual may be common knowledge to another. Let's just put it this way: I consider myself an average member, so if I came across something in my research that I said wow to, even after fifty-two years in the Church, I felt it deserved to be in this book. When I compiled *Unique Stories & Facts from LDS History*, I was definitely afraid that my definition of unique would turn out to be quite common to readers; nevertheless, I was extremely pleased (and relieved) at the feedback from numerous individuals as they spoke of the fascinating new facts they never knew before reading my book.

I hope you have as much fun answering the questions in *Mormon History 101* as I did compiling them.

ARTIFACTS AND ITEMS

1. What happened to the stone box that housed the golden plates for centuries on end?
   a. It broke up and washed to the base of the Hill Cumorah
   b. It filled in with dirt and debris—current location unknown
   c. It was taken by treasure seekers and sold
   d. The land owner eventually threw it into his stone property line

2. What did Martin Harris find when he went back to the Hill Cumorah with a shovel?
   a. Lots of rock
   b. Arrowheads dating to the last great battle between the Nephites and Lamanites
   c. Another stone box
   d. An old shoe

3. What would happen when "money diggers" found stone boxes or chests?
   a. The money diggers would become very rich
   b. The boxes or chests would move so that the money diggers could not find them again
   c. The angel Moroni would command the money diggers to bury the boxes back in the earth
   d. The seals on the boxes were so strong that the money diggers could not open them, and they gave up

4. What item did the Apostles carry constantly with them, including in the Nauvoo Temple, shortly after the death of the Prophet Joseph Smith?
   a. The Book of Mormon
   b. Hymn books
   c. Six-shooters
   d. Extra tithing envelopes

5. What did Joseph Smith carry on his person at all times to inform him if the plates were in danger?
   a. The Liahona
   b. The Urim and Thummim
   c. Hiram Page's seer stone
   d. Contact information to Palmyra's psychic

6. A St. Louis newspaper reported that two of the mummies that Joseph Smith purchased were the bodies of whom?
   a. Miriam and Aaron
   b. Caleb and Joshua
   c. Abraham and Joseph
   d. Pharaoh and Potiphar

7. While tracting in California in 1946, missionary Vern Thacker and his companion came across what?
   a. The original plans to the Nauvoo Temple
   b. Brigham Young's cane
   c. The golden plates
   d. The original angel that graced the top of the Nauvoo Temple

8. Just how accurate was the wood contraption that served as an odometer in Brigham Young's 1847 company?
   a. Off by 23 miles
   b. Off by 213 feet
   c. Off by 5.5 miles
   d. Off by 60 feet

9. What happened to the scrolls that were purchased with the Egyptian mummies by Joseph Smith during the Kirtland years?
   a. They were given back to the Egyptians
   b. They were burned in the great Chicago fire of 1871

    c.   Portions were found in a New York museum and later given to the Church

    d.   They were given to the angel Moroni

10. To understand this next fact and the significance of it, you must know that Symonds Ryder is the individual who apostatized from the Church due to the misspelling of his name on his mission call. Rather than being spelled R-y-d-e-r, his name was spelled R-i-d-e-r. Symonds was part of the mob that tarred and feathered Joseph Smith on March 24, 1832. What did his great-great-granddaughter donate to the Church?

    a.   The original rough draft of the Articles and Covenants (sections 20 and 22 of the Doctrine and Covenants)

    b.   The tar bucket that Symonds used the night Joseph Smith was tarred and feathered

    c.   An original copy of the Book of Mormon

    d.   An original Book of Commandments

ANSWERS

1. a. It broke up and washed to the base of the Hill Cumorah

From a *Chicago Times* interview with David Whitmer: "Three times has he [David Whitmer] been at the Hill Cumorah and seen the casket that contained the tablets and the seer-stone. Eventually the casket had been washed down to the foot of the hill, but it was to be seen when he last visited the historic place."

David Whitmer Interviews: A Restoration Witness, *Lyndon W. Cook ed. (Orem, Utah: Grandin Book, 1993), 7.*

2. c. Another stone box

Brother Harris then turned himself as though he had no more to say and we made ready to go. He then spoke again and said, "I will tell you a wonderful thing that happened after Joseph had found the plates: three of us took a notion to take some tools and go to the hill and hunt for some more boxes or gold or something, and indeed we found a stone box; we got quite excited about it; and dug quite carefully around it. We were ready to take it up, but behold, by some unseen power, it slipped back into the hill. We stood there and looked at it. One of us took a crowbar and tried to drive it through the lid to hold it; but it glanced and only broke one corner off of the box."

Ole A. Jensen, "Testimony of Martin Harris (One of the Witnesses of the Book of Mormon)," BYU, 1–6.

3. b. The boxes or chests would move so that the money diggers could not find them again

After this, on the 22nd of September, 1827, before day, Joseph took the horse and wagon of old Mr. Stowel[l], and taking his wife, he went to the place where the plates were concealed, and while he was obtaining them, she kneeled down and prayed. He then took the plates and hid them in an old black oak tree top which was hollow. Mr. Stowel[l] was at this time at old Mr. Smith's, digging for money. It was reported by these money-diggers, that they had found boxes, but before they could secure them, they would sink into the earth. A candid old Presbyterian told me, that on the Susquehannah flats he dug down to an iron chest, that he scraped the dirt off with his shovel, but had nothing with him to open the chest; that he went away to get help, and when they came to it, it moved away two or three rods into the earth, and they could not get it.

"Mormonism—II," Tiffany's Monthly 5 (August 1859): 163–70.

4. c. Six-shooters

"At this time, strong attempts are making to take the Twelve. It seems as though earth and hell are made to see the work of the priesthood proceeding so rapidly. The United States Marshall has been here for some time searching and laying in wait for the Twelve and some others. He searched the [Nauvoo] temple through but in vain. The brethren have had to disguise themselves and conceal themselves to escape them. The charge is treason. You may see the Twelve, etc. wherever they go with six shooter pistols in their pockets, but thus far they have been preserved and are ministering in the [Nauvoo] temple and teaching the way of life and salvation."

Joseph Fielding, Diary (1843–46), Church Archives in "They Might Have Known That He Was Not a Fallen Prophet"—The Nauvoo Journal of

Joseph Fielding," transcribed and edited by Andrew F. Ehat, BYU Studies
19 (Winter 1979).

The following took place in the Nauvoo Temple: "December 11,
1845. Thursday: At 1 o'clock Elder Orson Pratt came up into the rooms
while we were attending to washing and anointing. He had just returned
from his mission to the east and brought with him $400 worth of six
shooters."

An Intimate Chronicle: The Journal of William Clayton, *edited by*
George D. Smith (Salt Lake City: Signature Books, 1995).

5. b. The Urim and Thummim

"Joseph kept the Urim and Thummim constantly about his person,
by the use of which he could in a moment tell whether the plates were
in any danger."

Lucy Mack Smith, History of Joseph Smith *(Salt Lake City: Book-*
craft, 1979), 142.

6. c. Abraham and Joseph

The public press indicated that two of the mummies that Joseph
Smith purchased in 1835 were the mummified bodies of Joseph and
Abraham. It was necessary for Joseph Smith to put that rumor down
since neither Abraham nor Joseph was left buried in Egypt.

Commercial Bulletin and Missouri Literary Register, *St. Louis,*
Missouri, October 12, 1835.

7. a. The original plans to the Nauvoo Temple

The following story is in reference to the rebuilding of the Nauvoo
Temple:

> Only a couple of photographs exist of the original building;
> none gave a view of all sides of the temple. For the architects, recon-
> struction was boosted by access to the original William Weeks plans,
> which had been given to the Church in an unusual turn of events.
> Vern Thacker, an LDS Missionary in the California Mission in 1946,
> came across the William Weeks architectural plans:
> "While we were tracting on the outskirts of town one day, we
> both felt inspired to stop at a small home. A man named Leslie M.
> Griffin invited us in and told us that he was a descendant of William
> Weeks, the architect for the Nauvoo LDS Temple." The missionar-
> ies visited him several times to discuss the gospel. Nearing the end

of his mission, Elder Thacker made one last visit to Mr. Griffin who "excused himself for a few minutes and went into the back part of his house. He soon returned with a roll of what looked like poster paper about three feet long, ten inches in diameter, and secured with a rubber band. He explained that these were the original plans for the Nauvoo Temple and that they had been handed down in his family from his grandfather, William Weeks. He opened the bundle and showed the plans to us. The largest of the papers was a side view of the Temple exterior. Rolled inside of this piece were several other smaller drawings showing various views of the Temple." He asked Elder Thacker if on his way home he would carry "these plans to the headquarters of the Church in Salt Lake." The plans were delivered to the Church Historians Office 28 September 1948, photographed and secured in "a steel-locked safe."

Vern C. Thacker, "The Nauvoo Temple Architect's Drawings Lost and Found," 20 January 2000;

Heidi S. Swinton, Sacred Stone *(American Fork, Utah: Covenant, 2002), 144.*

8. d. Off by 60 feet

I am certain that most people have seen a picture of the odometer constructed by William Clayton or visited the Church Museum of History and have seen the original odometer used to measure the distance traveled each day by the Saints as they made their way to the Salt Lake Valley. This very crude odometer was constructed of wood gears and was attached to one of the covered wagons. One's initial assessment is that this contraption was far from accurate, judging by the crudeness of its appearance. The following might just astound you. It did me.

The pioneer odometer was invented by two men who made the initial trek to Utah in 1847 and was used by Brigham Young on one wagon to measure the distance from the Missouri River to the Great Salt Lake Valley. The difference between the measurements of this crude instrument and those made by government surveyors who later passed over the same route with more sophisticated instruments was only 60 feet!

The original odometer is now at the Church Museum of History in Salt Lake City.

Douglas F. Tobler and Nelson B. Wadsworth, The History Of The Mormons In Photographs And Text: 1830 To The Present *(New York: St. Martins Press, 1987), 129.*

9. c. Portions were found in a New York museum and later given to the Church

The following is in relation to the Egyptian scrolls that Joseph Smith purchased during the Kirtland years of the Church: "After the Prophet's death they, along with the mummies, were sold to non-Mormons and exhibited in various places, including Wood's Museum in Chicago. For years it was assumed that they all were destroyed in the great Chicago fire of 1871, but in 1967 eleven fragments were discovered in a New York museum and presented to the Church."

James B. Allen and Glen M. Leonard, The Story of the Latter-day Saints *(Salt Lake City: Deseret Book, 1992), 77.*

10. a. The original rough draft of the Articles and Covenants (sections 20 and 22 of the Doctrine and Covenants)

In 1959 Virginia Ryder Watters, great-great-granddaughter of Symonds Ryder, donated an original rough draft of the Articles and Covenants [Sections 20 and 22 of the Doctrine and Covenants] to the Historical Department via a Latter-day Saint high school student her husband knew. The document is titled "A commandment from God unto Oliver how he should build up his Church & the manner thereof." It concludes "A true copy of the Articles of the Church of Christ. O.C. [Oliver Cowdery]" ("Historical," 287, 290).

Arnold K. Garr, Donald Q. Cannon, and Richard O. Cowan, Encyclopedia of Latter-day Saint History *(Salt Lake City: Deseret Book, 2000), 51–52.*

AFRICAN AND NATIVE AMERICANS

1. How many African-American Saints entered the Salt Lake Valley with the first company of pioneers in the summer of 1847?
   a. 0
   b. 3
   c. 4
   d. 5

2. Who coined the phrase, "It is better to feed the Indians than to fight them?"
   a. Brigham Young
   b. Porter Rockwell
   c. William Penn
   d. Jim Bridger

3. When did the first man of African descent receive the priesthood?
   a. March 1836
   b. June 1978
   c. July 1978
   d. December 1850

4. Who was the first prophet to teach about priesthood and individuals of African descent?
   a. Alma
   b. Joseph Smith
   c. Noah
   d. Brigham Young

5. Throughout the 1800s, whenever the Native Americans in the Idaho-Utah area wanted to be preached to by either elders or members of the Church, they used a unique phrase to indicate their desire. What was this phrase?
   a. "Talk Brigham"
   b. "Preach the good word"
   c. "Spirit talk"
   d. "Whisper to my spirit"

6. Kanosh was the head Pahvant Ute Chief at the time the Saints entered the Salt Lake Valley. Who was Kanosh's father-in-law?
   a. Blackhawk
   b. Walkara (also known as Walker)
   c. Lot Smith
   d. Brigham Young

7. Walker Lewis was ordained to the priesthood in about 1843 or 1844, even though he was an African-American man. Who ordained him to the office of an elder?
   a. William Smith
   b. Sidney Rigdon
   c. John Taylor
   d. Willard Richards

8. Frank Warner, a full-blooded Northern Shoshone Indian, survived which massacre as an infant, even after receiving seven bullet wounds?
   a. Wounded Knee
   b. The Battle of Provo River
   c. The Bear River Massacre
   d. Custer's Last Stand

9. How many African-American Saints entered Winter Quarters in 1848?
   a. 2
   b. 12
   c. 21
   d. 34

10. On June 6, 1848, the Heber C. Kimball Company engaged in battle with the Omaha Indians at the meeting of the Elkhorn and Platte rivers. What did Dr. Jesse Brailey successfully use to defend himself?
    a. An umbrella
    b. A bowie knife
    c. A pot and pan
    d. A disguise to make him look like a woman

11. Arapeen, brother to Ute Chief Walkara, donated what to the Church after his baptism?
    a. 50 ponies
    b. All of the Ute tribal holdings
    c. 100 acres of land at the current site of the Manti Temple
    d. All of the stolen livestock and belongings of the Saints

ANSWERS

1. **b. 3**

Green Flake, one of the three African-Americans to enter the Salt Lake Valley with the first company of Saints, was born on the Jordan Flake plantation in Anson County, North Carolina. There are no known birth records for Hark Lay and Oscar Crosby, the two other African-Americans in the party.

Green Flake was born in approximately 1828. In 1841 he traveled with his owners, James Madison and Agnes Love Flake, to Kemper County, Mississippi, where the family cleared land for a farm. During the winter of 1843–44 Madison and Agnes were baptized as members of the Church and so was their servant Green. When the Flakes decided to join the main body of the church in Nauvoo, Green accompanied them. For a time he served as a bodyguard for Joseph Smith.

Leonard J. Arrington, "Black Pioneer Was Union Fort Settler," The Pioneer (SUP), September–October 1981; Ronald G. Coleman, "A History of Blacks in Utah, 1825–1910" (Ph.D. diss., University of Utah, 1980).

2. c. William Penn

At the time Box Elder was first settled, it was regarded as dangerous Indian territory, but Bishop Davis followed William Penn's advice of feeding the Indians instead of fighting them—a policy also taught and impressed upon the Saints by the wisdom of President Brigham Young. Following this maxim Bishop Davis won the hearts of the red men, and they were ever his friends. They used to call him "The Captain," and he was always able to get along with them except when they were on the warpath.

History of William Davis from a manuscript on file in the Brigham City, UT, city library; http://www.boap.org/

3. a. March 1836

Elijah Abel, an early black convert, pioneer, and missionary, was ordained an elder on March 3, 1836. Zebedee Coltrin ordained Elijah a seventy on December 20 that same year. In 1908, Joseph F. Smith stated his understanding that Joseph Smith himself declared Abel's ordination "null and void." President Smith offered no basis for that assertion. Abel did not believe that his ordination had ever been nullified. And twenty-nine years earlier, in 1879, Joseph F. Smith noted that Elijah Abel had two certificates identifying him as a seventy, one of them issued in Utah.

Jessie L. Embry, Black Saints in a White Church: Contemporary African American Mormons *(Midvale, Utah: Signature Books, 1994), 39; Excerpts from Council minutes August 26, 1908, Kimball Papers; Edward L. Kimball, "Spencer W. Kimball and the Revelation on Priesthood,* BYU Studies, *Vol. 47, no. 2 (2008), 8.*

4. d. Brigham Young

The first Church President to teach about the priesthood and "the Africans" was Brigham Young.

Journal History of the Church, *February 13, 1849, Church History Library.*

5. a. "Talk Brigham"

From the autobiography of August Adrainus Hjorth:

I helped in many ways during the Black Hawk War in Cache Valley. At one time I was sent out with two men to recover some workhorses the Indians had stolen. After a long ride, we went down into a gulch and made a fire and cooked our last bit of food. As we were wondering where to look next, a group of Indians surrounded us. One of our men was an old trapper and could speak their language. The Indians asked what we were doing there and were told we had come to find the horses they had stolen. They seemed very unfriendly. They started dragging dry timber and piled it up. They also put a long pole on the ground. We imagined they were going to burn us at the stake. However they tied a turkey buzzard on the end of the pole and began dancing around the pole after lighting their bonfire.

While all these preparations were going on, the chief and two other Indians came down in front of us and wanted us to talk to them. The interpreter talked to them a few minutes but they wanted us to "talk Brigham." (They wanted to hear about the Church.) I knew possibly half a dozen words in their language. I had never preached a sermon in my life; but when I stood upon my feet, the Spirit of the Lord came upon me with great power. I spoke for over an hour to those Indians in their language. When I sat down, the interpreter said, "Where did you learn to talk Indian?" What I had said seemed to please them, and they gave us some food; and we joined in their dance around the camp fire and slept among them all night unmolested. In the morning we were told that our horses were down the canyon a little way. We gathered them together and returned home. After I talked to the Indians, the Chief, Curley Bull, shook hands with me and called me "Topeke," which means pointed. I had talked to the point about the gospel.

Many years later these same Indians were given seats of honor in the Tabernacle at a conference session. Chief Curley Bull, then an old man, was among them. His grandson Frank, who spoke English, was their spokesman. Being especially interested in the Indians, I talked to them and told them some of my experiences in Cache Valley among the Indians and was informed by two or three of them that some of their relatives were killed in the Bear River Massacre (January 29, 1863). This Frank was only a small boy when I spoke to them in their own language years ago, but he remembered the incident and informed me that many of them were converted that night around the camp fire. Although a young and inexperienced man, I, with the aid of my Heavenly Father, had planted the seed of righteousness in the hearts of these Indians.

Chronicles of Courage, *Compiled by Lesson Committee (Salt Lake City: Daughters of Utah Pioneers, 1991), 192–93.*

6. **d. Brigham Young**

Believe it or not, Kanosh married Sally, the adopted Paiute daughter of Brigham Young.

Paul Pailla, "Kanosh." Utah History Encyclopedia, Allan Kent Powell ed. (Salt Lake City: University of Utah Press, 1994), 297–98.

7. **a. William Smith**

"Walker Lewis was ordained an elder by the Prophet Joseph Smith's brother William Smith in 1843 or 1844 in Lowell, Massachusetts."

Connell O'Donovan, "The Mormon Priesthood Ban and Elder Q. Walker Lewis," John Whitmer Historical Association Journal *26 (2006), 48, 82–95.*

8. **c. The Bear River Massacre**

His parents were Sagwitch and Tan-tapai-cci of the Northwestern Shoshone. Frank's actual name was Pisappih Timbimboo, and he was a two-year-old at the time of the Bear River Massacre on January 29, 1863. His body was riddled with seven bullet wounds but yet he survived. A few years later, he was adopted by the Amos Warner family and renamed Frank W. Warner. President John Taylor called him on a mission in 1880 to work among his own people. He served a second mission in 1914–15 working among the Sioux and Assiniboin Indians of Fort Peck, Montana.

Scott R. Christensen, Sagawitch: Shoshone Chieftain, Mormon Elder, 1822–1887 *(Logan, Utah: Utah State University Press, 1999); Frank W. Warner, "Missionary journal, November 1914–January 1915." Manuscript. LDS Church Archives, Salt Lake City.*

9. **d. 34**

In 1848 a group of Saints from Mississippi, 56 whites and 34 African-Americans, entered Winter Quarters on their way to the Salt Lake Valley.

Mormon Historical Studies, *Vol. 1, No. 1, Spring 2000, p. 44.*

10. **a. An umbrella**

On June 6, 1848, just west of Winter Quarters, where the Elkhorn River flows into the Platte, the Heber C. Kimball Company engaged in a battle with the attacking Omaha Indians. Four natives were killed and two of the Saints badly wounded. After the engagement the natives found a Dr. Jesse Brailey alone on the wrong side of the Elkhorn River.

Immediately one of the Indians raised and pointed his rifle at Dr. Brailey. All Jesse Brailey could do was raise his umbrella as if in the act of returning fire. Luckily, it worked. He was able to scare off the Omaha brave and buy enough time to join himself in the safety of the main body of the Saints.

Mormon Historical Studies, *Vol. 1, No. 1, Spring 2000, 44.*

11. b. All of the Ute tribal holdings

Arapeen was eventually baptized into the Church and donated all his possessions plus the Ute tribal holdings totaling over $155,000 to the Church. As much as the Church appreciated this act of faith, the property was never formally transferred.

Feramorz Y. Fox, "The Consecration Movement of the Middle 'fifties,'" Improvement Era, *February 1944, No. 2.*

AGRICULTURE AND EVERYDAY PIONEER LIFE

1. How much was the fine for killing a seagull shortly after the Saints arrived in the Salt Lake Valley?
    a. $5.00
    b. $1.00
    c. $0.50
    d. $2.50

2. What is the present-day location of the first planting of potatoes and turnips on the day the Saints entered the Salt Lake Valley in 1847?
    a. 300 South and North Temple
    b. 400 South and South Temple
    c. At the intersection of I-80 and I-215.
    d. 300 South and State Street

3. When Arocet Hale was working his wheat fields and saw the first group of gold-seekers enter the valley, he went to their camp. What was the first thing they desired to see?
    a. The Book of Mormon
    b. Gold dust
    c. Brigham Young
    d. The Mormon Tabernacle Choir

4. What was the fine for those who violated the "anti-bigamy law" signed by President Lincoln on July 8, 1862?
    a. 1 day in jail

b. $100 fine

c. $500 fine or five years' imprisonment or both

d. Exile to Canada

5. Prayer was a part of everyday pioneer life. What did the Saints in Hawaii pray for during construction of the temple there?
   a. For rain
   b. For lumber to continue building the temple
   c. For missionaries to find more converts to help build the temple
   d. For good weather to allow for construction of the temple

6. Jacob Hamblin mentions in his journal that while he and his family were sick and in need of water, someone came to tempt him. Who was it?
   a. A Methodist class minister
   b. Lilburn Boggs
   c. Satan
   d. The Missouri mob

7. According to his autobiography, how many pounds of potatoes did John Horner grow in California in 1853?
   a. 220 lbs.
   b. 2,200 lbs.
   c. 220,000 lbs.
   d. 22 million lbs.

ANSWERS

1. a. $5.00

"The most of the barley grain near the city was saved by immense flocks of seagulls which came and devoured the crickets. This was considered a Godsend and many escaped what might have been a severe famine. A fine of five dollars was placed upon the head of anyone that killed a seagull. One thing singular, the oldest mountaineers and trappers said that they never saw a seagull until after the Mormons settled this country."

Five dollars doesn't sound like much, but let me help you put this in perspective. Realize the average man worked for just a little more than a dollar a day. That same fine would be about $600–$800 today. Ouch!

Journal of Arocet Lucious Hale, Typescript, HBLL; http://www.boap.org/

2. d. 300 South and State Street

The first plot of potatoes and turnips, planted on the same day that the Saints entered the valley in 1847, was established at the present-day intersection of Third South and State Street in Salt Lake City. These were planted immediately after Brigham Young entered the valley at 11:45 in the morning. The plowing of the land actually happened on the previous day, July 23, 1847.

The Church News, March 10, 1990; http://historytogo.utah.gov/utah_chapters/pioneers_and_cowboys/index.html

3. b. Gold dust

In consequence of the scanty harvest of 1848, bread stuff and other provisions became very scarce. Many had to eat raw hides, dig segos and thistle roots for months. I was one of that number. The last of June, just before harvest, was the hardest time of 1849.

I will relate a little incident to show to our children and the rising generation how their parents suffered in the early days of 1847, 1848 and 1849. Lucas Hoagland moved my sister Rachel Lavory Hale late in the fall of 1848. Our families then consisted of five in number, Lucas and wife, my brother, Alma Helaman Hale, age ten, my brother Solomon Elephlet Hale, age seven, and myself. After Lucas married my sister Rachel, of course I had more help to sustain the family. It fell to my lot to attend to watering the wheat. We had two cows, luckily both giving milk. When I went to the field to water the wheat and fight the crickets, I used to drive one cow to the field with me at night, milk the cow, and strain the milk. As soon as it was cool, I would stir in two or three spoonfuls of moldy corn meal, set it over the campfire, make my porridge and go to bed. I did the same in the morning. This was better with the blessing of the Lord on it than boiled rawhide and thistle roots. For dinner, I would take my shovel and go out on the bench land and dig segos which were plentiful, thank the Lord.

While I was tending the wheat, Lucas was working around where he could get a little provisions for the family. He used to go to the Provo River with fishing parties, catch fish, salt and dry them. They were very good and considered a rarity.

I will relate a little incident to show how hard it was to get bread stuff. My wheat was heading out and commenced turning a little yellow. I thought I could glean a little out that would do to thresh and grind in a hand mill, which many did. I saw several going to Neff's Mill with small grists of corn that were rare in 1848. The thought struck me that I might be able to trade for some. I had a fine little saddle horse that Lucus Hoagland had told me to trade for bread stuff or edibles of any kind. I saddled up, went to the mill, and saw several there begging or trying to (some widows with families). I spoke to Neff and told him my situation. I offered him the horse, saddle and bridle (a new California Macheir [?] saddle for three pecks of corn meal, one peck to take home with me, one peck the next week, the third peck, the third week. Now for the answer. Said he, "You great booby, here trying to get three pecks of meal. There are women here begging for two quarts to take home with them to feed their little children." This anger hurt my feelings very badly. I thought of the situation I had left the family in in the morning, without a spoonful of anything to eat of bread stuff kind. Then I cried like a baby to be called a booby for trying to make an honest trade with the miller.

I continued fighting crickets until nearly night, when I heard a noise towards the mouth of Emigration Canyon, a little north of me. I looked and to my surprise, I saw a train of four- and six-horse wagons coming out of Emigration Canyon. This proved to be a company of the gold emigration, the first that arrived in the valley. I sprung to my horse and went across the bench into their camp. I was the first Mormon boy in their camp. They appeared to be very much excited over gold and the mines and asked many questions. What news from the gold Mines? Is there any more of the battalion boys come in? What news do they bring? Have you seen any? Have you got any gold? I had very little that Hoagland had given me to try and get a little bread stuff with. I let them see what gold I had. They were all excited in a minute and all had to see the gold dust. While they were looking at the gold dust, an old gentleman touched me on the shoulder and beckoned me to one side. Said he, "I have a span of young American colts, four years old. They have been worked on lead, and have pulled themselves down very poor." Said he, "I will give you that span of young horses, their harness and lead bars for your pony, saddle and bridle." I told him that I would go with him and see the horses. We went, and he showed me the horses. They were as he reckoned them to me. I thought of the trade I had offered the Miller Neff a few hours before. I thought of my sister and the little boys at home without anything to eat but a little milk and segos for supper.

Said I, "Could you spare me a few pounds of flour, a small piece of bacon, a quart of beans or any kind of vegetables?" "Come to the wagon and I will see what I can find." He got into the wagon, threw out a sack with eight or ten pounds of flour, ten pounds of bacon and by that time the boys had gotten supper. They invited me into the tent. There I ate the best supper that I ever ate, or relished the best. I had not tasted nice white bread and fried bacon for months. I led my horse to the city. When my sister Rachel saw flour and bacon, she wept for joy.

Gold emigration continued to come and they were willing to trade their poor stock for those that were in better condition. The gray horses that I got for the saddle pony brought me two yoke of oxen and wagons and a nice suit of clothes. This reminds me of a prophecy of President Heber C. Kimball two months before the gold emigration came into the valley. He prophesied that clothing would be cheaper in Salt Lake City than it was in New York City. We saw this prophecy come to pass. They were loaded too heavy to continue their journey and all had something to sell or trade, horses, harnesses or wagons, clothing, provisions, cooking utensils, stoves, tents, guns and ammunitions. This was considered a Godsend.

Journal of Arocet Lucious Hale, Typescript, HBLL; http://www.boap. org/

4. **c. $500 fine or five years' imprisonment or both**
    William Edwin Berrett, The Restored Church *(Salt Lake City: Deseret Book, 1973), 316.*

5. b. For lumber to continue building the temple

Due to the remoteness of the Hawaiian Island, construction often came to a standstill waiting on material. On one such occasion, Ralph Woolley, the temple contractor, knelt in prayer and supplicated his Heavenly Father for the needed material to continue construction on the Hawaii Temple. A few days later a severe storm hit, causing a freight ship to become lodged on the coral reef. The captain of the ship, realizing his dilemma, offered the load of lumber in his ship if the Saints helped him to get it off. This blessing resulted in the continuation of the temple construction.

Hyrum C. Pope, About the Temple in Hawaii *(Hawaii, 1919), 149–50.*

6. a. A Methodist class minister

I labored with the company of pioneers to prepare the way for the Saints through Iowa, after which I had the privilege of returning to Nauvoo for my family, which consisted of my wife and three children. I moved them out into Iowa, 200 miles, where I left them, and returned 100 miles to settlements, in order to obtain food and other necessaries.

I was taken sick, and sent for my family to return to me. My wife and two children were taken sick the day after their arrival. We found shelter in a miserable hut, some distance from water.

One day I made an effort to get some water for my suffering family, but failed through weakness. Night came on and my family were burning with fever and calling for water.

These very trying circumstances called up some bitter feelings within me. It seemed as though in this, my terrible extremity, the Lord permitted the devil to try me for just then a Methodist class leader came along, and remarked that I was in a very bad situation. He assured me that he had a comfortable house that I could move into, and that he had plenty of everything, and would assist me if I would renounce "Mormonism." I refused and he passed on.

I afterwards knelt down and asked the Lord to pity us in our miserable condition, and to soften the heart of someone to administer to us in our affliction.

About an hour after this, a man by the name of William Johnson came with a three gallon jug full of water, set it down and said: "I came home this evening, weary, having been working with a threshing machine during the day, but, when I lay down I could not sleep;

something told me that you were suffering for water. I took this jug, went over to Custer's well and got this for you. I feel now as though I could go home and sleep. I have plenty of chickens and other things at my house that are good for sick people. When you need anything I will let you have it." I knew this was from the Lord in answer to my prayer.

The following day the quails came out of the thickets, and were so easily caught that I picked up what I needed without difficulty. I afterwards learned that the camps of the Saints had been supplied with food in the same way.

James A. Little, Jacob Hamblin in Three Mormon Classics, *Preston Nibley, comp. (Salt Lake City: Bookcraft, 1988), 215–16.*

7. d. 22 million lbs.

Member John Horner tells of the success of his crop in the California gold fields:

He arrived home safely in the fall and in time to take the place he had left in the firm of J. M. Horner & Co., to sell our large crop now ready for market. We continued our energetic and prosperous career buying more lands and farming them ourselves, or letting them to tenants until our potato crop reached the enormous quantity of twenty two million pounds in 1853. We had also in that year fifteen hundred acres of wheat and barley, besides cabbages, tomatoes and onions in quantities. California had not only supplied herself with vegetables this (1853) year, for the first time, but she produced a large surplus which could not be sold, and was never sent to market.

Journal of John M. Horner; http://www.boap.org/

BAPTISMS, OTHER CHURCH ORDINANCES, THE GIFTS OF THE SPIRIT, AND TITHING

1. Where was the largest gathering of spectators at an LDS baptism?
   a. The River Ribble in Preston, England
   b. The Jordan River in Salt Lake City
   c. City Creek in Salt Lake City
   d. Lake Erie at Fairport, Ohio

2. Rebaptism was a common occurrence in early Church history. Why did this practice end?
   a. Too many members catching colds
   b. Members saw this as an easy way to repent
   c. Jesus was only baptized once, so once should be good enough
   d. The General Authorities realized, as stated in Ephesians 4:5, that there is "one Lord, one faith, one baptism"

3. During the Kirtland years, what was seen at the place of baptism during the night hours?
   a. A pillar of fire
   b. A pillar of light
   c. Angels with torches
   d. Two moons

4. George Reynolds's parents denied permission for him to be baptized when he was nine years old. What caused George to sneak behind their backs to be baptized at age fourteen?
   a. The Elders were leaving his area, so he knew there would not

be priesthood authority left to baptize and he didn't want to lose his chance

b. Brigham Young was leaving for Salt Lake City, and George didn't want to be left behind

c. He was afraid the Savior's Second Coming would take place before he was baptized

d. He desired to be the 3,000th person baptized into the Church

5. After a mob discovered that one of their meeting attendees, Gilbert Belnap, was a spy for the Prophet Joseph, what did Brother Belnap bless to ensure his escape?
   a. His feet
   b. The sheriff and his deputies
   c. The mob
   d. His horse

6. While consecrating oil in the Kirtland Temple, what did Zebedee Coltrin see?
   a. The finger of God
   b. Joseph Smith caught up in vision
   c. A heavenly choir of angels
   d. Fire encircling him and the other men participating

7. What was a typical language heard while one was speaking in tongues?
   a. Spanish
   b. Canadian
   c. A Native American language
   d. Hebrew

8. True or false? In the early Church, consecrated oil was administered internally.

9. How many people did Levi Hancock (an early member of the Quorum of the Seventy and a spiritual leader in the Mormon Battalion) help baptize and confirm in one meeting?
   a. 11
   b. 37
   c. 71
   d. 86

10. When Joseph Smith healed Elsa Johnson's arm, there was a doctor present. The doctor did not believe it was Joseph that healed the arm but rather attributed it to something else. What was it?
    a. Nothing was ever wrong with Elsa Johnson's arm—she was faking the injury
    b. When Joseph stretched out her arm, perspiration began to flow, causing the cords to loosen
    c. The power of Satan
    d. The doctor's prescription, given two weeks earlier, to rub tobacco leaves over the affected arm

11. What did the Maori king prophesy in 1879 would happen to his people?
    a. Missionaries preaching in pairs would teach his people
    b. His people would never lack for food
    c. Their gods would smile favor on them
    d. They would outgrow their island in New Zealand and would continue to grow and prosper in Australia

12. In a blessing to Arocet Hale, Heber C. Kimball prophesied what to him?
    a. He would never be sick with the ague again
    b. He would become a very wealthy man
    c. He would become a father to many
    d. He would serve a mission in another country

13. True or false? Heber J. Grant saw in council the Savior, Heber's father, and the Prophet Joseph Smith.

14. What ordinance had to be performed twice for Spencer W. Kimball due to a question of legitimacy the first time it was done?
    a. Ordination to deacon
    b. Receiving the gift of the Holy Ghost
    c. Baptism
    d. Ordination to the office of elder

15. To date, how many prophets have been baptized in City Creek in Salt Lake City?
    a. 1
    b. 2

c. 3
d. 4

16. True or false? The location of Gordon B. Hinckley's baptism is well known among Church historians.

17. Who did Joseph Smith claim broke the bread portion of the sacrament in fist-sized pieces?
    a. The Nephites
    b. Jesus and his Apostles
    c. Melchizedek and Abraham
    d. Enoch and his people

18. What request did Joseph Smith have of Cordelia Morley Cox in 1844?
    a. That she consider a mission
    b. That she would assist Emma with the housework around the Mansion Home
    c. That she would work in his store
    d. That she would be his plural wife

19. The prophecy and curse that the Prophet Joseph Smith placed upon John C. Bennett is similar to the curse of what other person?
    a. Laman
    b. King Noah
    c. Cain
    d. Lemuel

20. How did Henry Bishop once pay his tithing?
    a. He did work for the Indians
    b. He worked at the tithing yards
    c. He worked on Salt Lake City streets
    d. He took food to widows in the valley

21. According to the journal of Douglas Todd Sr., in 1887 the name *tithing* was changed to what?
    a. The Lord's pay
    b. Donations
    c. The Lord's tenth
    d. Fire insurance

22. Before leaving the Salt Lake Valley, Sister Flake used what to settle her tithing account?
    a. Livestock
    b. Her grown children's old toys
    c. Her servant
    d. Produce from her garden

23. What experience did Harrison Burgess claim to have?
    a. An out-of-body experience
    b. A visitation from the angel Moroni
    c. A vision similar to Joseph Smith's first vision
    d. A visit from the Three Nephites

24. Where was Harrison Burgess when he viewed Joseph Smith in vision with the Savior?
    a. The Nauvoo Temple
    b. Joseph Smith's Red Brick Store in Nauvoo
    c. The Newell K. Whitney Store
    d. The Kirtland Temple

25. Who appeared to Brigham Young in vision to show him the Salt Lake Valley as the end destination of the Saints?
    a. The Savior
    b. Joseph Smith Jr.
    c. Moses
    d. Joseph Smith Sr.

26. What did Philo Dibble see as he was traveling at night from Lexington to Far West, Missouri?
    a. An army marching through the sky
    b. Joseph Smith being pursued by a mob
    c. An aura over Far West
    d. The New Jerusalem

27. When Diantha Clayton viewed Joseph Smith in vision, what did she desire of him?
    a. A blessing
    b. A promise that he would reserve a place for her in heaven
    c. A kiss
    d. For him to tell her the future of her family

28. Who did Anthon Lund (the Manti Temple President and General Authority) say appeared to a brother in the cemetery in Ephraim, Utah?
    a. His deceased relatives, asking him to do their temple work
    b. His deceased parents, reminding him of his commitment and obligation to do the work for their family
    c. His deceased parents, reminding him to water the garden
    d. His deceased wife, reminding him that he had better not remarry

29. What did a voice tell Chapman Duncan he would find if he traveled to the West?
    a. Sage brush
    b. Little water
    c. My Church
    d. Native Americans

30. What incident caused Drusilla Hendricks to clean her house?
    a. The mob was getting ready to push her out of her home, and she didn't want it said that she was a poor housekeeper
    b. Her family had eaten the last of the food in the house, and now all that was left was to die
    c. The First Presidency was coming over for a visit
    d. Her mother-in-law was coming over for dinner

31. Prior to joining the Church, at what point did Jacob Hamblin know the Book of Mormon was true?
    a. After three years of reading and investigation
    b. After he read it and prayed about it
    c. The moment he touched it
    d. The moment the missionaries told him it was true

32. True or false? Consecrated oil was placed on injured body parts during pioneer times.

33. Why did the Spirit whisper to Wilford Woodruff not to get on a steamer at Pittsburgh while traveling with a group of Saints to the Salt Lake Valley in 1850?
    a. It was a slow steamer and they would make better time by getting on another vessel

b. The captain was an ex–mob member, and he had planned mischief for the group of Saints
c. The steamer was not river-worthy
d. The steamer was going to burn

34. While on a mission in West Virginia, how did Jacob Hamblin obtain reliable information that the Prophet and Hyrum had been shot?
    a. The people he was teaching informed him
    b. The Spirit whispered that a man standing across the street was an elder and to ask him
    c. He read about it in a newspaper
    d. The local mob told him

35. One time Jacob Hamblin decided to cut short a camping trip up the canyon with his family because he knew they were being watched by Indians. When his wife asked how he knew, what was Jacob's reply?
    a. "I've heard one too many owl hoots in broad daylight"
    b. "The same way I know the gospel is true"
    c. "By the smoke signals off in the distance"
    d. "The horses are fidgeting, and they never do that unless something is going to happen"

36. What did Lucy Mack Smith hear the Spirit say when she asked Heavenly Father why Joseph and Hyrum were killed?
    a. "I have taken them to myself, that they might have rest"
    b. "It's Brigham Young's turn to lead this Church"
    c. "I have taken them to me to see if the Saints will follow those things that Joseph and Hyrum taught"
    d. "They have finished their work that I have given them"

37. The practice of sealing individuals in the Church to General Authorities was eventually discontinued. Of the four choices below, three are reasons why it was discontinued. What are the three reasons?
    a. The General Authorities could not always be present at the sealing in the temple, which was a requirement
    b. Concerns about what would happen if a General Authority fell away from the church

c.	Not everyone met the General Authorities' standards for people that they would want to be sealed to

d.	The belief that all who would have accepted the gospel, even though they may not have had this knowledge in life, will become heirs to celestial glory gave renewed hope

38.	What three things was nonmember Christina Forsgren shown in vision?

a.	A man with three books, her future husband, and the fact that she would be in a plural marriage situation

b.	The next President of Sweden, her future husband, and her future children

c.	A man telling her that the Lutheran Church was not correct, Joseph Smith, and the Book of Mormon

d.	Herself moving to America, living in Nauvoo, and pulling a handcart

39.	Why was Sarah Delight Stocking baptized while she and her family were en route from Nauvoo to Winter Quarters?

a.	Baptism for immersion
b.	Baptism for the dead
c.	Baptism for healing
d.	Rebaptism

40.	True or false? When baptism for the dead was first introduced to the Church, it was not uncommon for female proxies to be baptized for males and vice versa.

ANSWERS

**1.	a. The River Ribble in Preston, England**

The record for most people attending a baptism could very well be Sunday July 23, 1837, when Elder Heber C. Kimball baptized nine individuals in the River Ribble in Preston, England, in the presence of 8,000 curious bystanders.

Truth Will Prevail: The Rise of The Church of Jesus Christ of Latter-day Saints in the British Isles, 1837–1987 *V. Ben Bloxham, James R. Moss, and Larry C. Porter, eds. (Cambridge: Cambridge University Press, 1987).*

2. b. Members saw this as an easy way to repent

It ended after the October conference in 1897, when George Q. Cannon preached that too many Saints saw this as an easy way to repent.

James B. Allen and Glen M. Leonard, The Story of the Latter-day Saints, *second edition (Salt Lake City: Deseret Book, 1992), 430–31.*

3. b. A pillar of light

As told by early Church member Philo Dibble:

> "I will here observe that about the time of which I write, there were many signs and wonders seen in the heavens above and in the earth beneath in the region of Kirtland, both by Saints and strangers. A pillar of light was seen every evening for more than a month hovering over the place where we did our baptizing. One evening also, as Brother William Blakesley and I were returning home from meeting, we observed that it was unusually light, even for moonlight; but, on reflection, we found the moon was not to be seen that night. Although it was cloudy, it was as light as noonday, and we could seemingly see a tree farther that night than we could in the day time."

"Early Scenes in Church History," Four Faith Promoting Classics, Philo Dibble Autobiography *(Salt Lake City: Bookcraft, 1968), 74–96.*

4. c. He was afraid the Savior's Second Coming would take place before he was baptized

George Reynolds was a member of the First Council of the Seventy and secretary to five presidents of the Church. While being raised in England, he became friends with a member of the Church. At age nine he desired baptism, but because of his young age he had to have his parents' consent, which they refused to give. George continued to attend church for a few years when he became fearful that the Savior's Second Coming would take place before he could be baptized. Therefore, at the age of fourteen (1856), he went to a branch where he was unknown and was baptized the following Sunday.

Bruce A. Van Orden, George Reynolds: Prisoner for Conscience' Sake *(Salt Lake City: Deseret Book, 1992).*

5. d. His horse

The following is in reference to Gilbert Belnap being chased by the mob from Carthage to Nauvoo after it was discovered that he was a spy for the Prophet Joseph.

> I afterward sat in council with delegates from different parts of the country and secured the resolutions passed by that assembly. I then returned in safety to Nauvoo, but not without a close pursuit by those demons in human shape, uttering the most awful imprecations, and bawling out to meet almost every jump to stop or they would shoot. My greatest fear was that my horse would fall under me. I thought of the instance of David Patton [Patten] administering to a mule which he was riding when fleeing before a similar band of ruffians. I placed my hands on either side of the animal and as fervently as I ever did, I prayed to God that his strength might hold out in order that I might bear the information which I had obtained to the Prophet. There were no signs of failure in accomplishing this purpose until just opposite the tomb. My horse fell on his side in the mud. This seemed to be a rebuke for me for urging him on to such a tremendous speed. We were entirely out of danger and covered with mud by reason of the fall. I rushed into the presence of the Prophet and gave him a minute detail of all that had come under my observation during that short mission.

Autobiography of Gilbert Belnap, Typescript, HBLL; http://www. boap.org/

6. a. The finger of God

> In Kirtland Temple, I [Zebedee Coltrin] have seen the power of God as it was in the day of Pentecost! and cloven tongues as of fire have rested on the brethren and they have spoken with other tongues as the spirit gave them utterance. I saw the Lord high and lifted up and frequently throng the solemn assemblies, the angels of God rested on the temple, and we heard their voices singing heavenly music. At another time when consecrating some oil, we saw visibly the finger of God enter the mouth of the bottle.

Minutes of High Priest Meeting, Spanish Fork, Utah, February 5, 1870.

7. c. A Native American language

The following from the autobiography of Jesse Crosby while living on his father's farm in western New York:

Many others followed the example, and a branch of the Church was organized [1838]. The Holy Ghost was poured out insomuch that many were healed of their infirmities, and prophesied, some saw visions, others spoke in different languages by the gift and power of God as on the day of Pentecost. The language or dialect of various tribes of the American Indians was spoken, and that too by persons who had never spoken with an Indian in their lives. I will own, that though I believed, I was astonished, but will add that I have since traveled among various tribes of Indians in the central and uncultivated parts of America and have recognized not only the language, but the gesture and very manner in which it was spoken.

One may inquire why it was that the spirit of God dictated these individuals to speak in the language of these wandering outcasts. Oh! here is the mystery that the world hath not seen. These are a remnant of Israel, the descendants of Joseph, and heirs to the promises made to their fathers; see Book of Mormon.

Autobiography of Jesse W. Crosby, Typescript, HBLL; http://www .boap.org/

John Corrill sheds more light on this subject:

I attended several meetings, one of which was the laying on of hands for the gift of the Holy Ghost, which, I thought, would give me a good opportunity to detect their hypocrisy. The meeting lasted all night, and such a meeting I never attended before. They administered the sacrament, and laid on hands, after which I heard them prophesy and speak in tongues unknown to me. Persons in the room, who took no part with them, declared, from the knowledge they had of the Indian languages, that the tongues spoken were regular Indian dialects, which I was also informed, on inquiry, the persons who spoke had never learned. I watched closely and examined carefully, every movement of the meeting, and after exhausting all my powers to find the deception, I was obliged to acknowledge, in my own mind that the meeting had been inspired by some supernatural agency. The next day I returned home, satisfied that the evil reports were not true, and spent about six weeks more in the further investigation of the subject.

John Corrill, A Brief History of the Church of Christ of Latter Day Saints (Commonly Called Mormons, Including an Account of their Doctrine and Discipline, with the Reasons of the Author for Leaving the Church) *(St. Louis, n.p., 1839).*

8. True

The following is from Benjamin Brown, who lived during the Nauvoo years of the Church. Read how he administers the oil to the one to be healed. "The oil arriving, we administered some to her internally, in the name of the Lord, when she arose without assistance"

Autobiography of Benjamin Brown; http://www.boap.org/

9. c. 71

"Spring has come. I go to the West, I went through Cleveland, Ohio holding meetings along the way. Went through Elina into Brownhelm where we held meetings and baptized and confirmed seventy-one (71) at one meeting from under my own hand. I felt so happy and blessed. We then returned to Rome."

Autobiography of Levi Hancock, Typescript, HBLL; http://www.boap. org/

10. b. When Joseph stretched out her arm, perspiration began to flow, causing the cords to loosen

The Methodist minister in this story was none other than Ezra Booth, one of the first apostates in the Church. It was because of this healing that he decided to join the Church. But this isn't what makes the story interesting; rather it's the doctor's reasoning of why Joseph was able to heal Elsa Johnson. Philo Dibble relates the following in his autobiography:

> When Joseph came to Kirtland his fame spread far and wide. There was a woman living in the town of Hiram, forty miles from Kirtland, who had a crooked arm, which she had not been able to use for a long period. She persuaded her husband, whose name was [John] Johnson, to take her to Kirtland to get her arm healed.
>
> I saw them as they passed my house on their way. She [Elsa Johnson] went to Joseph and requested him to heal her. Joseph asked her if she believed the Lord was able to make him an instrument in healing her arm. She said she believed the Lord was able to heal her arm.
>
> Joseph put her off till the next morning, when he met her at Brother [Newel K.] Whitney's house. There were eight persons present, one a Methodist preacher, and one a doctor. Joseph took her [Elsa Johnson] by the hand, prayed in silence a moment, pronounced her arm whole, in the name of Jesus Christ, and turned and left the room.

The preacher asked her if her arm was whole, and she straightened it out and replied: "It is as good as the other." The question was then asked if it would remain whole. Joseph hearing this, answered and said: "It is as good as the other, and as liable to accident as the other."

The doctor who witnessed this miracle came to my house the next morning and related the circumstance to me. He attempted to account for it by his false philosophy, saying that Joseph took her by the hand, and seemed to be in prayer, and pronounced her arm whole in the name of Jesus Christ, which excited her and started perspiration, and that relaxed the cords of her arm.

"Early Scenes in Church History," Four Faith Promoting Classics, Philo Dibble Autobiography *(Salt Lake City: Bookcraft, 1968), 74–96.*

11. a. Missionaries preaching in pairs would teach his people

Even before missionaries first visited the Maori people of New Zealand, their king (King Tawhiao), in 1879 prophesied that men from the true church would come and visit them. He said, "They will not come to you and return to European accommodations but they will stay with you, talk with you, eat with you, and abide with you." Paora Potangaroa, a spiritual leader among the Maori elaborated by explaining that these ministers of the true religion would travel in pairs and always raise their right arm to the square while performing holy ordinances. It's interesting to note that the first missionaries to the Maoris began teaching in 1881 with the first branch being established in 1883.

Brian W. Hunt, Zion in New Zealand, 1854–1977 *(Temple View, New Zealand: Church College of New Zealand, 1977), 9; Matthew Cowley, "Maori Chief Predicts Coming of LDS Missionaries,"* Improvement Era, *September 1950, 696.*

12. a. He would never be sick with the ague again

I will here relate a prophecy of President Kimball upon my head. I was taken sick before my father, with the ague and fever shook about two hours in the forenoon and a burning fever in the afternoon. I was not able to take care of myself. Brother Kimball came into the tent where I was laying on the bed. He said, "Arocet, where are your cattle that your father moved into this camp with?" Father nor me has seen an ox or cow for two weeks. Says he, "Arocet, if you will get up tomorrow morning and go and hunt cattle enough to move your wagons out of this camp, up to Winter Quarters, you never shall have another ague shake as long as you live." I tried to make some excuse but no good. Some of the brethren and sisters had gathered around the tent door, hearing them talk to me. Said he, "Will you go?" I said, "I will try to go." Brother Kimball spoke to Uncle James Allred [written above line: then administered to me]. Said he, "Brother Allred, you have a horse, saddle and bridle here tomorrow by eight o'clock. Brother Hale is going to get cattle enough to take his wagons up to Winter Quarters, at my camp, a distance of twelve miles."

In the morning, Brother Allred was there with the riding animals which were little white mules which belonged to some of the brethren that had come from Texas that year. I started according to agreement. They watched me as far as they could see me. Some of the women said that I would never return alive. Some found fault with Brother Kimball [for] sending a boy as sick as I was alone to hunt cattle. I rode to Mosquito Creek, five miles. I was nearly checked for water. I corralled my mule to the creek and had a good drink of water, laid back on the bank to rest me, and fell asleep. I did not wake up until after dark. I found my mules a short distance below on the creek. I caught the mules and was thinking what to do. I had not seen any camps as yet on the creek. While thinking what course to pursue, I heard a dog bark up the creek. I crawled on to the mule and started up the creek. I soon found a camp and told them who I was and what I was after. The man was a little acquainted with father. They took me in and took care of me and in the morning sent a boy with me. The third day I found three oxen and one cow. I returned to camp. Some were surprised to see me. Others were soon inquiring about Brother Kimball. Previously I told them I had not had an ague shake once I left them. I then and there bore my testimony that if there ever was a prophet of God on this earth, that President Heber C. Kimball was one.

Journal of Arocet Lucious Hale, Typescript, HBLL; http://www.boap. org/

13. True

The following story is in reference to the revelation received by President John Taylor on October 13, 1882 calling George Teasdale and Heber J. Grant to the holy Apostleship.

An experience of Elder Heber J. Grant a few months later gives some background to this revelation. Heber reported that for the first few months of his apostleship he felt that he was not qualified to be a special witness of the Savior. While traveling on the Navajo reservation in northern Arizona in February 1883, helping establish the Church among the Indians, Elder Grant told his companions he wanted some time by himself and took a different route to their destination. He later recounted what happened as he rode:

"I seemed to see, and I seemed to hear, what to me is one of the most real things in all my life, I seemed to see a Council in heaven. I seemed to hear the words that were spoken. . . . In this Council the Savior was present, my father [Jedediah M. Grant] was there, and the Prophet Joseph Smith was there. They discussed the question that a mistake had been made in not filling those two vacancies and that in all probability it would be another six months before the Quorum would be completed, and they discussed as to whom they wanted to occupy those positions, and decided that the way to remedy the mistake that had been made in not filling these vacancies was to send a revelation. It was given to me that the Prophet Joseph Smith and my father mentioned me and requested that I be called to that position. I sat there and wept for joy. . . .

". . . From that day I have never bothered, night or day, with the idea that I was not worthy to stand as an Apostle."

B.H. Roberts, Life of John Taylor *(Salt Lake City: Bookcraft, 1963), 349–51, as quoted in* Conference Report, 4 Apr. 1941, pp. 4–5.

14. c. Baptism

"Because of concerns that his first baptism, which took place in the family bathtub, might not have been performed appropriately, Spencer W. Kimball [was] baptized a second time, in the Union Canal in Thatcher, Arizona."

Richard Neitzel Holzapfel et al., On This Day in the Church *(Salt Lake City: Eagle Gate, 2000), 194.*

15. d. 4

"Heber J. Grant [was] baptized in City Creek in Salt Lake City, the second of four future Presidents of the Church to be baptized in the same location."

Richard Neitzel Holzapfel et al., On This Day in the Church *(Salt Lake City: Eagle Gate, 2000), 108.*

16. False

"In April of 1919, Gordon B. Hinckley [was] baptized at eight years of age, location unknown. Of the site he [stated]: 'It's the only secret I have left! It was done by proper authority in a proper place.'"

Richard Neitzel Holzapfel et al., On This Day in the Church *(Salt Lake City: Eagle Gate, 2000), 83.*

17. b. Jesus and his Apostles

The following from Zebedee Coltrin:

> The salutation as written in the Doctrine and Covenants [D&C 88:136–41] was carried out at that time, and at every meeting, and the washing of feet was attended to, the sacrament was also administered at times when Joseph appointed, after the ancient order; that is, warm bread to break easy was provided and broken into pieces as large as my fist and each person had a glass of wine and sat and ate the bread and drank the wine; and Joseph said that was the way that Jesus and his disciples partook of the bread and wine. And this was the order of the church anciently and until the church went into darkness. Every time we were called together to attend to any business, we came together in the morning about sunrise, fasting and partook of the sacrament each time, and before going to school we washed ourselves and put on clean linen.

Minutes, Salt Lake City School of the Prophets, October 3, 1883.

18. d. That she would be his plural wife

The following from the autobiography of Cordelia Morley Cox

> While I am on earth and able to write with the pen in my own hand, I will give to my children and my children's children, a testimony that I know that God lives and will bless all those who wish to do his will. I was baptized when eight years old. I always tried to bear a good name and follow the teachings of my parents and those whose right it was to rule over me. In the spring of forty-four [1844], plural marriage was introduced to me by my parents from Joseph Smith, asking their consent and a request to me to be his wife. Imagine if you can my feelings, to be a plural wife, something I never thought I ever could. I knew nothing of such religion and could not accept it. Neither did I.
>
> In June 1844, Joseph Smith was martyred and it was a time of mourning for all. After Joseph Smith's death, I was visited by some of his most intimate friends who knew his request and explained to me this religion, counseling me to accept his wishes for he now was gone

and could do no more for himself. I accepted Joseph Smith's desire and in 1846, January 27, was married to your father in the Nauvoo Temple. While still kneeling upon the altar, my hand clasped in his, now his wife, he gave his consent and I was sealed to Joseph Smith for eternity. I lived with your father and loved him. I was satisfied with the course I had taken. I had three little girls with him. I took comfort [they were] born under the new and everlasting covenant. I had not doubted. I thought if one principle taught by Joseph Smith was true, all he taught must be true. I was sincere in my belief and had never doubted the truth of what I had accepted. Still, I had no testimony for myself of the truth of such a principle and became acquainted with the trials and hardships of such a life but was satisfied and contented in the course I had taken. I had three little girls born under the new and everlasting covenant. I loved them and took good care of them.

The Latter-day Saints were preparing to leave and come to Utah. We lived in a settlement where as the Mormons moved away, the Gentiles would buy the improvements until our family was left quite alone with the outside world. Then they began to persecute us. Your father was taken into a Gentile court and tried for breaking laws of the land by living with more than one wife. I had a true companion; her husband was mine also. We were driven from our home in the dead of winter. They told us our religion was false and we had been deceived. I had no one to go to for knowledge or for comfort. I began to worry and to wonder if I had in these ears been so deceived. I longed for a testimony from my Father in Heaven, to know for myself whether I was right or wrong. I was called a fallen woman. The finger of scorn was pointed at me. I felt that it was more than I could endure and in the humility of my soul, I prayed that I might have a testimony from him who knows the hearts of all. One night I dreamed. I thought I was in the midst of a multitude of people. President Young arose and spoke to the people. He then said there would be a spirit go around to whisper comfort in the ear of everyone. All was silent as death as I sat. Then the spirit came to me and whispered in my ear these words, "Don't ever change your condition or wish it otherwise," for I was better off than thousands and thousands of others. This brought peace to my mind and I have felt satisfied ever since. The Lord has been my guide; in Him I put my trust. I am thankful that I have been true to the covenants I have made with my Father in Heaven. I am thankful for my children that have been given to me. I pray that God will accept us all, and blessed to come forth through a glorious resurrection and receive a crown of eternal life in His kingdom.

Cordelia Cox, Autobiography (1823–1909), Holograph HBLL. See also http://www.boap.org/

19. c. Cain
John C. Bennett was the first mayor of Nauvoo.

The Prophet Joseph predicted a curse on John C. Bennett. He told him if he did not repent of his sins and sin no more, the curse of God Almighty would rest upon him, that he would die a vagabond upon the face of the earth, without friends to buy him. He told him that he stunk of women. In the year 1850, President Young was speaking about the matter. He said that he had watched the life of John C. Bennett. Bennett went to California in the great gold fever excitement, that Bennett died in one of the lowest slums of California, that he was dragged out with his boots on, put into a cart, hauled off, and dumped into a hole, a rotten mass of corruption. This prediction or prophecy came to pass as well as many others that I heard the Prophet Joseph make.

Journal of Arocet Lucious Hale, Typescript, HBLL; http://www.boap. org/

20. a. He did work for the Indians
Savalla Bishop Melville wrote the following: "Grandfather followed his trade of smithing, was delegated by the Church to do work for the Indians for tithing."

Autobiography of Henry William Bigler, Typescript HBLL, http:// www.boap.org/

21. b. Donations
"March 15, 1887: Attended Theological class. Restoration was spoken upon. Bishop gave us to understand that no more tithing would be received. The name must be changed to donations. Wondered if the changing of the name would affect many."

The next entry from Brother Todd's journal may explain why his bishop wanted to change the name of tithing to "donations": "January 29, 1888: Pres. Smoot and counselor spoke to us today. Bro. S. said that no more than 25% of the tithing was paid. We will eventually rule the nations if but 12 men remain true."

Excerpts from the Journal of Douglas M. Todd Sr.

22. c. Her servant

Green Flake was one of three African Americans to enter the Salt Lake Valley with the first group of Saints in 1847. He might also be the first human being to be used as a means of paying tithing. Green Flake's owners joined the Church during the winter of 1843–44 in North Carolina. At the time of the Flakes' coming into the Church, they gave all their slaves freedom if they so desired. Green Flake chose to stay with them. After Brother Flake passed away, his wife decided to leave the Salt Lake Valley and move to California. Before leaving she settled her tithing, using Green Flake as partial payment. Benefitting from his services for a short time, Brigham Young soon gave him his freedom.

Richard S. Van Wagoner and Steven C. Walker, A Book of Mormons *(Salt Lake City: Signature Books, 1982).*

23. c. A vision similar to Joseph Smith's first vision

The following is related by Harrison Burgess:

> On the third Sabbath in May while speaking to a congregation I declared that I knew that the Book of Mormon and the work of God were true. The next day while laboring in the field something seemed to whisper to me, "Do you know the book [Book] of Mormon is true?" My mind became perplexed and darkened, and I was so tormented in spirit that I left my work and retired into the woods. The misery and distress that I there experienced cannot be described. The tempter all the while seemed to say, "Do you know that the Book of Mormon is true?"
>
> I remained in this situation about two hours. Finally I resolved to know, by exercising faith similar to that which the Brother of Jared possessed, whether I had proclaimed the truth or not, and commenced praying to the God of Heaven for a testimony of these things. Suddenly a glorious personage clothed in white stood before me and exhibited to my view the plates from which the Book of Mormon was taken.

Harrison Burgess, "Labor in the Vineyard," Twelfth Book of the Faith Promoting Series, *65–66.*

24. d. The Kirtland Temple

The following vision is recorded by Harrison Burgess:

> The Lord blessed His people abundantly in that Temple [i.e. the Kirtland Temple] with the Spirit of prophecy, the ministering

of angels, visions, etc. I will here relate a vision which was shown to me. It was near the close of the endowments. I was in a meeting for instruction in the upper part of the Temple, with about a hundred of the High Priests, Seventies and Elders. The Saints felt to shout "Hosannah!" and the Spirit of God rested upon me in mighty power and I behold the room lighted up with a peculiar light such as I had never seen before. It was soft and clear and the room looked to me as though it had neither roof nor floor to the building and I beheld the Prophet Joseph and Hyrum Smith and Roger Orton enveloped in the light: Joseph exclaimed aloud, "behold the Savior, the Son of God." Hyrum said, "I behold the angels of heaven." Brother Orton exclaimed, "I behold the chariots of Israel."

All who were in the room felt the power of God to that degree that many prophesied, and the power of God was made manifest, the remembrance of which will remain with me while I live upon the earth.

Harrison Burgess, "Labors in the Vineyard," Twelfth Book of the Faith Promoting Series, *67.*

25. b. Joseph Smith Jr.

We look around today and behold our city clothed with verdure and beautified with trees and flowers, with streams of water running in almost every direction, and the question is frequently asked: "How did you ever find this place?" I answered; we were led to it by the inspiration of God. After the death of Joseph Smith, when it seemed as if every trouble and calamity had come upon the Saints, Brigham Young, who was President of the Twelve, then the presiding Quorum of the Church, sought the Lord to know what they should do, and where they should lead the people for safety, and while they were fasting and praying daily on this subject, President Young had a vision of Joseph Smith, who showed him the mountain that we now call Ensign Peak, immediately north of Salt Lake City, and there was an ensign fell upon that peak, and Joseph Said, "Build under the point where the colors fall and you will prosper and have peace." The pioneers had no pilot or guide, none among them had never been in the country or knew anything about it. However, they travelled under the direction of President Young until they reached this valley. When they entered it President Young pointed to that peak, and, said he, "I want to go there." He went up to the point and said, "This is Ensign Peak. Now, brethren, organize your exploring parties, so as to be safe from Indians; go and explore where you will,

and you will come back every time and say this is the best place."
They accordingly started out exploring companies and visited what
we now call Cache, Malad, Tooele, and Utah valleys, and other parts
of the country in various directions, but all came back and declared
this was the best spot.

Journal of Discourses, *26 vols. (Liverpool: Latter-day Saint's Book
Depot, 1854–86), 13:85–86.*

26. d. The New Jerusalem

The following is an experience as recorded by Philo Dibble during
the tumultuous Missouri years:

> On my return home, when I got to Liberty, midway between
> Lexington and Far West, I concluded I would travel from there home
> by night, as it was very warm during the day. The road led through
> a strip of timber for four miles, and after that across a prairie for
> twenty miles.
>
> When I had traveled about two-thirds of the way across the
> prairie, riding on horseback, I heard the cooing of the prairie hens.
> I looked northward and saw, apparently with my natural vision, a
> beautiful city, the streets of which ran north and south. I also knew
> there were streets running east and west, but could not trace them
> with my eye for the buildings. The walks on each side of the streets
> were as white as marble, and the trees on the outer side of the marble
> walks had the appearance of locust trees in autumn. This city was
> in view for about one hour-and-a-half, as near as I could judge, as I
> traveled along. When I began to descend towards the Crooked River
> the timber through which I passed hid the city from my view. Every
> block in this mighty city had sixteen spires, four on each corner,
> each block being built in the form of a hollow square, within which
> I seemed to know that the gardens of the inhabitants were situated.
> The corner buildings on which the spires rested were larger and
> higher than the others, and the several blocks were uniformly alike.
> The beauty and grandeur of the scene I cannot describe. While view-
> ing the city the buildings appeared to be transparent. I could not
> discern the inmates, but I appeared to understand that they could
> discern whatever passed outside.
>
> Whether this was a city that has been or is to be I cannot tell.
> It extended as far north as Adam-ondi-Ahman, a distance of about
> twenty-eight miles. Whatever is revealed to us by the Holy Ghost
> will never be forgotten.

Early Scenes in Church History, Four Faith Promoting Classics,

Philo Dibble Autobiography, *(Salt Lake City: Bookcraft, 1968), 74–96.*

27. c. A kiss

The following is an incident that William Clayton's wife experienced:

> 16 July 1845, Wednesday: Evening I went to see Diantha. We walked out some together. She seemed to feel very bad about something which passed during her visit this afternoon. When we returned to her home I saw that her mind was affected and she was likely to have another fit of mental derangement. I tried to persuade her to go to bed but she was unwilling, but I finally got her mother to make her a bed down stairs and we put her to bed by force. Soon as she got laid down she began to toss about and rave as if in great pain which seemed to increase until she was perfectly out of her mind and raging. She tore her hair and I then held her which required all the force I had got to hold her hands. She continued about three quarters of an hour in this distressing situation and about half past 10 Sister Farr went and called Brother Farr. He came down and laid hands on her and rebuked the evil spirit and commanded it to leave her in the name of the Lord. She immediately calmed down and seemed to fall into a mild sleep. Soon after she commenced talking or rather answering questions. She seemed to be in the world of spirits on a visit, and about the first she conversed with was Brother Joseph (Smith) and the conversation seemed to be on the subject of the massacre. She then appeared to go and visit a number of her dead relatives who invariably enquired about their relatives on the earth. The answers she gave were literally facts as they exist. She then enquired for William Smith's wife Caroline. She was soon taken to her and entered into conversation. Caroline asked about William, how he acted, how he felt towards the Twelve, what was his course, how her two girls were and whether he had got married. To all these interrogatories she answered in the nicest manner, avoiding carefully anything which would wound Caroline's feelings. She then enquired for Sister Richards and soon met with her. It seemed by her answers that Sister Richards asked how the Doctor felt when she left him, how his children were, and whether Lucy lived with him, all which she answered correctly. She then visited Wm. Snow's first wife and conversed about Wm. and his daughter and father. She then appeared to go back to Brother Joseph and Hyrum Smith and father Smith. Joseph asked about Emma and the children and how the Twelve and Emma felt towards each other and all which she

answered wisely but truly. He also asked about Lydia and gave her some instructions for Lydia. He asked about me [William Clayton] and told her I was a good man. When she parted with her friends she always bid the "good-bye" but when she parted with Joseph she said, "I am not in the habit of kissing men but I want to kiss you" which she appeared to do and then said "farewell." She then seemed to start back for home. She appeared all the time in a hurry to get back. She said she would like to tarry but she could not leave father and mother and another, but she would soon return and bring them with her and then she would tarry with them. She conversed about two hours in this manner and seemed overjoyed all the time. A pleasant smile sat on her countenance which continued after she awoke. It was one of the most interesting and sweet interviews I ever witnessed, and a very good spirit seemed to prevail all the time. I left about 1 o' clock apparently much composed and comparatively free from pain.

William Clayton's Nauvoo Diaries and Personal Writings; http://www.boap.org/

28. a. His deceased relatives, asking him to do their temple work

The second President of the Manti Temple, Anthon H. Lund, relates the following story:

"I remember one day in the temple at Manti, a brother from Mount Pleasant rode down to the temple to take part in the work, and as he passed the cemetery in Ephraim, he looked ahead (it was early in the morning), and there was a large multitude all dressed in white, and he wondered how that could be. Why should there be so many up here; it was too early for a funeral, he thought; but he drove up and several of them stepped out in front of him and they talked to him. They said, 'Are you going to the temple?' 'Yes.' 'Well, these that you see here are your relatives and they want you to do work for them.' 'Yes,' he said, 'but I am going down today to finish my work. I have no more names and I do not know the names of those who you say are related to me.' 'But when you go down to the temple today you will find there a record that give our names.' He was surprised. He looked until they all disappeared, and drove on. As he came into the temple, Recorder Farnsworth came up to him and said, 'I have just received records from England and they all belong to you.' And there were hundreds of names that had just arrived, and what was told him by these persons that he saw was fulfilled. You can imagine what joy came to his heart, and what testimony it was to him that the Lord wants this work done.

Temples to the Most High, *N.B. Lundwall, comp. (Salt Lake City: Bookcraft, 1966), 116.*

29. c. My Church

Born in the state of New Hampshire, Grafton Co. town of Bath July 1st, 1812. Being decided that I was in consumptive state of health, I designed to travel by the way of Louisville, Kentucky, and New Orleans to Demerara, South America, left home September 1832 to recover my health. I took passage at Louisville for New Orleans on the steamboat Warrior. The day before she left the ward, while laying in my state room, the following sentence was spoken to me in an audible voice. I was not asleep. "If you proceed your journey you contemplate, you will surely die, but if you will go to the western border of the state Missouri by the border of the Lamanites you shall live there and you shall find my Church." I looked around to see who spoke to me. An audible voice answered, "The Holy Ghost." The confirmation which I experienced of the fact that it was the Holy Ghost, I cannot here describe, only that it was I felt a perfect assurance of the spirit of God which affected my whole system. I had not fear or doubt of the heavenly message.

Autobiography of Chapman Duncan, Typescript, HBLL; http://www. boap.org/

30. b. Her family had eaten the last of the food in the house, and now all that was left was to die

The story of Drusilla Hendricks is typical of the Quincy experience. Her husband, James, had been shot in the neck in the Battle of Crooked River and had to be carried about on a stretcher. The family arrived in Quincy on 1 April and secured a room "partly underground and partly on top of the ground." Within two weeks they were on the verge of starving, having only one spoonful of sugar and a saucerful of corn meal to eat. Drusilla made mush out of it. Thinking they would eventually starve, she washed everything, cleaned their little room thoroughly, and waited for the worst. That afternoon Rubin Allred came by and told her he had had a feeling they were out of food, so on his way into town he'd had a sack of grain ground into meal for them. Two weeks later they were again without food. Drusilla remembered, "I felt awful, but the same voice that gave me comfort before was there to comfort me again, and it said, hold on, the Lord will provide for his Saints." This time Alexander

Williams arrived at the back door with two bushels of meal on his shoulder. He told her he had been extremely busy but the Spirit had whispered to him that "Brother Hendricks' family is suffering, so I dropped everything and came by."

Drusilla Doris Hendricks, "Historical Sketch of James Hendricks and Drusilla Dorris Hendricks," Typescript, LDS Historical Department, Salt Lake City, 22–23.

31. c. The moment he touched it

The following from the life of Jacob Hamblin:

In February, 1842, a neighbor called at my house and told me that he had heard a "Mormon" Elder preach. He asserted that he preached more Bible doctrine than any other man he had ever listened to, and that he knew what he preached was true. He claimed that the gospel had been restored to the earth, and that it was the privilege of all who heard it to know and understand it for themselves.

What this neighbor told me so influenced my mind, that I could scarcely attend to my ordinary business.

The Elder had left an appointment to preach again at the same place, and I went to hear him. When I entered the house he had already commenced his discourse. I shall never forget the feeling that came over me when I saw his face and heard his voice. He preached that which I had long been seeking for; I felt that it was indeed the gospel.

The principles he taught appeared so plain and natural, that I thought it would be easy to convince any one of their truth. In closing his remarks, the Elder bore testimony to the truth of the gospel.

The query came to my mind: How shall I know whether or not these things are so, and be satisfied? As if the Spirit prompted him to answer my inquiry, he again arose to his feet and said: "If there is anyone in the congregation who wishes to know how he can satisfy himself of the truth of these things, I can assure him that if he will be baptized, and have hands laid upon him for the gift of the Holy Ghost, he shall have an assurance of their truth."

This so fired up my mind, that I at once determined to be baptized, and that too, if necessary, at the sacrifice of the friendship of my kindred and of every earthly tie.

I immediately went home and informed my wife of my intentions.

She told me that if I was baptized into the "Mormon" Church, I need not expect her to live with me anymore.

The evening after the Elder had preached I went in search of him, and found him quite late at night. I told him my purpose, and requested him to give me a "Mormon Bible." He handed me the Old and New Testaments.

I said, "I thought you had a new Bible. He then explained about the coming forth of the Book of Mormon, and handed me a copy of it.

The impressions I received at the time cannot be forgotten. The spirit rested upon me and bore testimony of its truth, and I felt like opening my mouth and declaring it to be a revelation from God.

On the 3rd of March, 1842, as soon as it was light in the morning, I started for a pool of water where [?] had arranged to meet with the Elder, to attend to the ordinance of Baptism. On the way, the thought of the sacrifice I was making of wife, of father, mother, brothers, sister and numerous other connections, caused my resolution to waver.

As my pace slackened, some person appeared to come from above, who, I thought, was my grandfather. He seemed to say to me, "Go on, my son; your heart cannot conceive, neither has it entered into your mind to imagine the blessings that are in store for you, if you go on and continue in this work."

I lagged no more, but hurried to the pool, where I was baptized by Elder Lyman Stoddard.

It was said in my confirmation, that the spirits in prison greatly rejoiced over what I had done. I told Elder Stoddard my experience on my way to the water.

He then explained to me the work there was for me to do for my fathers, if I was faithful, all of which I believed and greatly rejoiced in.

On my way home, I called at the house of one of my neighbors. The family asked me if I had not been baptized by the "Mormon" Elder. I replied that I had. They stated that they believed what he preached to be the truth, and hoped they might have the opportunity of being baptized.

The following day Elder Stoddard came to my house, and told me that he had intended to leave the country, but could not go without coming to see me. For what purpose he had come, he knew not.

I related to him what my neighbors had said. He held more meetings in the place, and organized a branch before leaving.

When my father learned that I had joined the "Mormons," he said he thought he had brought up his children so that none of them would ever be deceived by priestcraft; at the same time he turned from my gate, and refused to enter my house.

Other relatives said that my father knew better than to be deceived as I had been. I answered them by predicting that, much as he knew, I would baptize him into the Church before I was two years older.

All my relatives, except one brother, turned against me, and seemed to take pleasure in speaking all manner of evil against me. I felt that I was hated by all my former acquaintances. This was a great mystery to me.

I prayed to the Lord and was comforted. I knew that I had found the valuable treasure spoken of by our Savior, and I was willing to sacrifice all things for it.

My wife's father took great pains to abuse and insult me with his tongue. Without having any conception how my prediction would be fulfilled, I said to him one day, "You will not have the privilege of abusing me much more." A few days after he was taken sick, and died.

Soon after the death of her father, my wife asked me, good-naturedly, why I did not pray in the house or with her. I replied that I felt better to pray by myself than I did before unbelievers. She said that she was a believer; that her father had appeared to her in a dream, and told her not to oppose me anymore as she had done; and that he was in trouble on account of the way he had used me. Soon after this she was baptized, which was a great comfort to me.

In the autumn of 1842, Elder Stoddard returned to the country where I lived, to labor in the ministry, and ordained me an Elder.

About the same time my wife was taken very sick. By her request, I administered to her, and she was immediately healed. I visited my father and told him that signs followed the believer, as in the days of the apostles; that I was a believer, and had been ordained an Elder in the Church of Jesus Christ of Latter-day Saints, and that the signs followed my ministrations.

He ordered me out of his house for believing such nonsense. I went out, reflecting as to whether or not I had done wrong in predicting that I would baptize him in less than two years.

Sometime after this he was taken sick, and I went to see him. My mother told me he had the spotted fever, and that there was no hope of his recovery. She believed he was dying, and so it appeared to me; but I thought that God could and would save him if I prayed for him.

I retired to a private place, and prayed to the God of Abraham to have mercy on my father and heal him, that he might have an opportunity of obeying the gospel.

It was a moonlight night, and when I returned to the house my mother stood at the door. She spoke to me very kindly, and said:

"Jacob, the fever has left your father; he has spoken and wants to see you."

As I approached him he said, "The fever has left me, and your mother says that you came to me and went away again. What has made such a sudden change? Do you know?"

I answered that I had prayed for him, that I was a believer in the gospel of the Son of God, and in the signs following those that believe.

"Well," said he, "if it is the gospel, I would like to know it; but if it is priestcraft, I want nothing to do with it."

Soon after the sickness of my father, I sold my home, gathered up my effects and started for Nauvoo, Hancock Co., Illinois.

In passing my father's house I found him quite well, and he desired me to remain over night. He showed much interest in the principles of the gospel, and, when I left his house in the morning, the Spirit manifested to me that my father and his household would yet accept the truth. . . .

. . . . The following winter I assisted in guarding the Saints in and around the city of Nauvoo. My brother Obed lived about thirty miles out in the country. He was taken sick, and sent for me to come and see him.

On arriving at his house, I found that he had been sick nearly three months, and that doubts were entertained of his recovery. I anointed him with holy oil in the name of the Lord Jesus, laid on hands, and prayed for him, and told him that he should recover, which he did immediately.

This occurrence had much influence on my parents. They both attended the following April conference. At its close, my father asked me if I did not wish to baptize him and my mother. As they were both desirous that I should do so, I baptized them in the Mississippi river, on April 11th, 1845.

My father told me that it was not any man's preaching that had convinced him of the truth of the gospel, but the Lord had shown it to him in night visions. Said he, "It is your privilege to baptize your parents, for you have prayed for them in secret and in public; you never gave them up; you will be a Joseph to your father's house."

James A. Little, Jacob Hamblin in Three Mormon Classics, *Preston Nibley, comp. (Salt Lake City: Bookcraft, 1988), 214.*

32. True

"When we got to Cash Cave we met father and Brother David Pettigrew going back to the bluff for us. So father returned with us to the valley. While we were going down East Canyon Creek mother's foot got caught in between the box and wagon tongue and broke the toe at the upper joint; but the skin was not broken. So father anointed her foot there and administered to her and it was healed quite soon."

Autobiography of Mosiah Hancock, Typescript, BYU-S; http://www.boap.org/

Another interesting story related to blessing with oil is found in the missionary journal of Oliver Huntington:

Thursday, August 3rd and Friday the 4th, we spent principally in reading, however in the course of the day we went over to Mr. Lewis', about 40 rods distant and there found one Mr. Millard, one of the devil's minute men, standing like a soldier of no sense at all to fight against truth and reason. He said he knew all about Mormonism and what it sprang from, it sprang from masonry or the death of Morgan, that Mormon was derived from the word Morgan. He said he could speak in tongues and prophesy to him.

So he said he would prophesy in the name of the Lord Jehovah that Mormonism did spring from the death of Morgan.

I then asked him if he laid hands on the sick. He said his boy was sick last night, and he laid hands on him anointing him with oil, also with salt and vinegar and he got better right off.

Autobiography of Oliver B. Huntington, Typescript, HBLL, http://www.boap.org/

The following is a blessing that Dwight Harding, a bodyguard to the Prophet Joseph Smith, received: "Dwight took seriously ill and his life was despaired of, but Phebe [his wife] prayed that his life might be spared, and sent for the elders. In the blessing, they asked the Lord to be mindful of Dwight, and he was promised that he would recover and take his family to the Salt Lake Valley to be among the Saints. He was also promised that he would live another twenty years. He lived twenty years and a few days after that blessing."

Kathryn H. Burrell, "Pioneers of Faith, Courage, and Endurance,"

Chronicles of Courage: Daughters of Utah Pioneers *(Salt Lake City: Utah Printing Company, 1991), 2:80.*

33. d. The steamer was going to burn

> While returning to Utah in 1850, with a large company of Saints from Boston and the east, on my arrival at Pittsburg, I engaged a passage for myself and company on a steamer to St. Louis. But no sooner had I engaged the passage than the Spirit said to me, "Go not on board of that steamer, neither you nor your company."
>
> I obeyed the revelation to me, and I did not go on board, but took another steamer.
>
> The first steamer started at dark, with two hundred passengers on board. When five miles down the Ohio River it took fire and burned the tiller ropes, so that the vessel could not reach the shore, and the lives of nearly all on board were lost either by fire or water. We arrived in safety at our destination, by obeying the revelation of the Spirit of God to us.

Leaves from My Journal, *Preston Nibley, comp. (Salt Lake City: Bookcraft, 1988), 102–103.*

34. b. The Spirit whispered that a man standing across the street was an elder and to ask him

The following story is from Jacob Hamblin's mission to Pennsylvania, Virginia, and Maryland:

> The way appeared to be opening up for a good work to be done in that country, when, about the 4th of July, news reached me that the Prophet, about whom I had preached so much, had been shot by a mob when confined in jail. I did not believe the report until I offered to preach to those who were gathered around me in the small town of Mechanicsburg. They manifested a spirit of exultation, and a feeling of deep gloom passed over me. I felt more like weeping than preaching.
>
> I concluded to hunt up my companion, from whom I was then separated. For this purpose I started for Hagerstown, where I hoped to find him, or learn of his whereabouts.
>
> I had traveled about a mile when I came to a cross road, and the Spirit whispered to me, "Stop here, and Brother Myers will soon be along." I remained on the spot about ten minutes, when I saw him coming, with his hat in one hand and his valise in the other. He did not believe that the Prophet was killed.

We journeyed together to Lightersburg. After meeting and passing many people, the Spirit indicated to us that a man on the opposite side of the street was an Elder in Israel. It proved to be a Latter-day Saint Elder, who had reliable information of the murder of the Prophet Joseph and the Patriarch Hyrum Smith. He also informed us that the Elders who were abroad were all called home.

James A. Little, Jacob Hamblin in *Three Mormon Classics, Preston Nibley, comp. (Salt Lake City: Bookcraft, 1988), 210.*

35. b. "The same way I know the gospel is true"

I settled, with my father and brothers, in Tooele Valley, thirty-five miles west of Salt Lake City. The people built their houses in the form of a fort, to protect themselves from the Indians, who frequently stole their horses and cattle. Men were sent against them from Salt Lake City, but all to no purpose. The Indians would watch them during the day, and steal from them at night.

This kind of warfare was carried on for about three years, during which time there was no safety for our horses or cattle. We had a military company, of which I was first lieutenant. I went with the captain on several expeditions against the thieves, but without accomplishing much good. They would watch our movements in the canyons, and continually annoy us.

At one time, I took my wife three miles up a canyon, to gather wild fruit while I got down timber from the mountain. We had intended to remain over night, but while preparing a place to sleep, a feeling came over me that the Indians were watching with the intention of killing us during the night.

I at once yoked my oxen, put my wife and her babe on the wagon, and went home in the evening. My wife expressed surprise at my movements, and I told her that the Indians were watching us. She wished to know how I knew this, and asked if I had seen or heard them. I replied that I knew it on the same principle that I knew that the gospel was true.

The following day I returned to the canyon. Three Indians had come down on the road during the night, and robbed a wagon of a gun, ammunition and other valuables. One of them, from the size of the track, must have been an Indian known as "Old Big Foot." I thanked the Lord that He had warned me in time to save my wife and child, as well as myself.

I'll now fast forward to a year later. "Afterwards, when trying to make peace with these Indians, 'Big Foot' told me, that himself and party had laid their plans to kill me and my wife and child, the summer before when in Pine Canyon, had we remained there over night."

James A. Little, Jacob Hamblin in Three Mormon Classics, *Preston Nibley, comp. (Salt Lake City: Bookcraft, 1988), 220–21, 224.*

36. a. "I have taken them to myself, that they might have rest"

"I had for a long time braced every nerve, roused every energy of my soul and called upon God to strengthen me," said Mother Smith, "but when I entered the room and saw my murdered sons extended both at once before my eyes and heard the sobs and groans of my family and the cries of 'Father! Husband! Brothers!' from the lips of their wives, children, brothers, and sisters, it was too much; I sank back, crying to the Lord in the agony of my soul. 'My God, my God, why hast thou forsaken this family!'" In reply Mother Smith heard a voice say to her, "I have taken them to myself, that they might have rest."

Lucy Mack Smith, History of Joseph Smith by His Mother, *Preston Nibley ed. (Salt Lake City: Bookcraft, 1956), 324.*

37. a, b, and d

Most Latter-day Saints are aware of the early church practice of adoptions to General Authorities. Many converts did not always have parents that were receptive to the church, and since it is important that individuals be sealed into a family unit, this then was the catalyst to perform the adoption. What may not be quite so familiar are the reasons this practice was phased out.

Gradually the practice of adoption gave way to the more natural principle of being sealed to one's own family—for several reasons. It was seldom convenient for Church leaders to be in attendance, as required, for temple adoptions. Furthermore, some leaders fell away from the Church, leaving confusion and dismay in the minds of their adopted families. More important, the emerging understanding of the doctrine that "all who have died without a knowledge of this gospel, who would have received it if they had been permitted to tarry, shall be heirs of the celestial kingdom" (D&C 137:7) gave renewed hope for all ancestors, regardless of their faith and condition in this life.

Arnold K. Garr, Donald Q. Cannon, and Richard O. Cowan, Encyclopedia of Latter-day Saint History *(Salt Lake City: Deseret Book, 2000), 10.*

38. a. A man with three books, her future husband, and the fact that she would be in a plural marriage situation

Christina Ericka Forsgren, had been converted to the gospel in a remarkable manner. Born in Gefle, Sweden, she had been trained in the faith of the Lutheran Church from infancy. As she grew to womanhood, however, she became dissatisfied with this church and prayed the Lord would show her the true path of salvation. One Sabbath Day in church, she had an open vision in which it was made known to her that the Lutheran, or State church, was a man-made church without divine authority, and that God did not acknowledge it. In the same vision she was shown that on a certain day a man would come to her with three books and that all who believed and accepted the things written in those books would be saved. In fulfillment of this vision on the fifth day of July, 1850, Elder John Eric Forsgren, a long lost brother visited her as a missionary of the Mormon Church and preached the gospel to her, making her acquainted with the three books—the Bible, the Book of Mormon and the Doctrine and Covenants!

Among other visions, she saw in her native land of Gefle, Sweden, a vision of her future husband, and that she would enter into the sacred principle of plural marriage. This had its fulfillment when she met Bishop Davis in the year 1853, for she recognized in him at once, the man shown to her in vision as her husband.

History of William Davis from a manuscript on file in the Brigham City, UT, city library. http://www.boap.org/

39. c. Baptism for healing

Sarah Delight Stocking Woodruff, fifth wife of Wilford Woodruff, shared this experience shortly after the Stocking family left Nauvoo en route to Winter Quarters:

During the journey Sarah's mother became ill with cholera and died. Wrapped in a sheet and covered with a thick bark from a nearby tree, her body was placed in the earth and covered with dirt and rock. The cholera epidemic was increasing, and the sick were not recovering. Sarah was very ill, and pleaded with her father to baptize her in the river, explaining that she knew if he would do so she would be made well, but if he did not, she would die. Her father decided to do so as she asked, although he was fearful her death might be hastened as a result of the baptism. He carried the child in a chair to the riverbank. News spread through the camp, and many of the company gathered to witness the ceremony. Some remonstrated with him, but he explained Sarah's faith was strong, and he must comply with her wishes. She was taken in his arms into the water where he baptized her three times. After the third immersion she was healed and walked from the water unaided.

Daughters of Utah Pioneers, Chronicles of Courage *(Salt Lake City: Utah Printing Company, 1991), 2:143.*

40. True

In this dispensation the first public mention of baptism for the dead was, according to the Prophet Joseph Smith's own declaration, made during the Prophet's sermon at the funeral of Seymour Brunson on 15 August 1840. (It seems apparent that he had been contemplating the subject for a time.) After the funeral service, a widow named Jane Nyman, to whom the Prophet had referred in his sermon, was baptized vicariously for her deceased son in the Mississippi River—the first occasion of the performance of the ordinance in modern times. In early days proxies were baptized for individuals regardless of gender (JD, 5:85), but now females stand as proxies only for females, and males only for males.

Arnold K. Garr, Donald Q. Cannon, and Richard O. Cowan, Encyclopedia of Latter-day Saint History *(Salt Lake City: Deseret Book, 2000), 76.*

BUILDINGS AND MONUMENTS

1. President Woodruff solicited Cyrus Dallin, a nonmember, to sculpt the angel Moroni on top of the Salt Lake Temple. Why did Cyrus initially refuse the offer?
   a. He did not like the Church
   b. He did not believe in angels
   c. The Church and Cyrus could not agree on a price
   d. He did not believe in the Book of Mormon, and therefore, Moroni could only be a mythical character

2. Who tried to put out the fire in the Nauvoo Temple in 1848?
   a. The Nauvoo Volunteer Fire Department
   b. A combined effort of member and nonmember residents of Nauvoo
   c. Porter Rockwell, Ephraim Hanks, and Lot Smith
   d. Lewis Bidamon (the man Emma Smith remarried)

3. How many days did it take to move the shaft stone of the Joseph Smith memorial 6 miles?
   a. 1 day
   b. 12 days
   c. 20 days
   d. 1 month

4. What happened to Brother James as he was taking a load of lumber from the canyon to the construction site at the Logan Temple?
   a. He was robbed of his load by the natives

b. He rolled the load over into the Logan River and survived even though he was trapped underwater for half an hour

c. He sold the lumber and kept the money

d. He used the lumber for his tithing

5. What did one nonmember do to enter the Logan Temple at the time of the dedication?

a. She paid the security guard to pass by into the temple

b. She disguised herself to look like President John Taylor's wife

c. She crawled through an open window

d. She purchased a member's temple recommend for $1

6. What area of the Salt Lake Temple was built with stone quarried from the same quarry as the Manti Temple?

a. The decorative tablets on the west and east ends of the temple

b. The capstone

c. The corner stones

d. The steps leading up to the east door

7. What year did the foundation of the Salt Lake Temple finally reach ground level?

a. 1851

b. 1859

c. 1867

d. 1875

8. What building housed the Dramatic Company, which was organized in 1850 in Salt Lake City?

a. The Bowery on the temple lot

b. Brigham Young's home

c. The Gardo House

d. The basement of Heber C. Kimball's home

9. It is said that Brigham Young left marks in the pulpit at the St. George Tabernacle due to the fervor of his speeches and a freewheeling cane. This is true. When did the first such mark appear?

a. Two months after the temple dedication, when Brigham was calling the Saints to repentance

b. One year after the temple dedication, as he was reprimanding the Saints for driving away the Natives in the area

c. At the temple dedication, in which he told the Saints he

wasn't satisfied with their efforts yet

  d. One week after the temple dedication, over his indignation of neighbors not loving their neighbors

10. Joseph Fielding referred to the newly completed Nauvoo temple as what?
  a. Heavenly
  b. Gothic
  c. Corinthian
  d. Doric

ANSWERS

1. b. He did not believe in angels

The Salt Lake Temple is the first temple to be graced with an angel identified as Moroni. Cyrus Dallin was solicited by President Woodruff to design a statue that could be placed on the 210-foot central east spire of the temple. What is interesting in this situation is that Cyrus was not a member of the Church and at first refused the offer saying he "didn't believe in angels." Undaunted, President Woodruff told Cyrus before he finalized his decision that he consult with his LDS mother. Dallin's mother was able to convince him to do the work by stating, "Why do you say that? [not believe in angels] You call me your 'angel mother.'" She encouraged him to study LDS scripture for inspiration. This study led to the formation of a neoclassical angel in robe and cap, standing upright with a trumpet in hand. The original 40-inch plaster model was completed by 4 October 1891 and exhibited at the Salt Lake Fair. A full-size model (12 feet 5 inches) was sent to Salem, Ohio, where the statue was hammered out of copper and covered with 22-karat gold leaf.

J. Michael Hunter, "I Saw Another Angel Fly," Ensign, Jan. 2000, 30.

2. d. Lewis Bidamon (the man Emma Smith remarried)

"Emma and her new husband, Lewis Bidamon, profited handsomely from tours of Nauvoo. Nevertheless, once the temple burned in 1848 the couple's salary was drastically cut to what Lewis describes as, 'one-fourth the custom [this refers to business] it previously had.' It's also interesting to note that at the time of the Nauvoo Temple fire Lewis worked hard at trying to put it out, but to no avail."

William E. Berrett and Alma P. Burton, Readings in LDS Church History, *3 vols. (Salt Lake City: Deseret Book, 1955), 2:87.*

3. c. 20 days

"The shaft stone for the Joseph Smith Memorial in Sharon, Vermont is 38½ feet long and was cut from a sixty ton block. To move the shaft stone the six miles from the railhead to the site took twenty days."

Church History in the Fulness of Times *(Salt Lake City: The Church of Jesus Christ of Latter-day Saints, 1993), 476.*

4. b. He rolled the load over into the Logan River and survived even though he was trapped underwater for half an hour

As the Saints willingly sacrificed time and money to build the temple, God's power was witnessed in the preservation of many lives, including that of nineteen-year-old Brother James, who, in the words of Nolan P. Olsen, "had loaded up about two tons of lumber and headed downstream toward the temple. . . . All went well for a short distance, until the wagon wheel hit a soft spot. The river bank caved in, dropping the two wheels and throwing Brother James on the bottom of the stream, with his big load upside down on top of him. It took the workmen nearly a half hour to break the binding and to roll the wagon and lumber from the river. Brother James had been underwater for this full length of time. They laid his body on the bank, covered it with a blanket and told one of the boys to get on a horse and come to Logan to tell the parents what had happened to their son.

Before the horse could be bridled, the blanket began to move and Brother James was up on his feet. Evidently his wind had been knocked out as his load went over, and he had not breathed for thirty minutes, and had no water in his lungs. The ice cold water had slowed his body processes, and he had no brain or bodily damage of any kind. He was none the worse for the experience, and reloaded his wagon and brought it on down to the temple.

Chad S. Hawkins, The First 100 Temples *(Salt Lake City: Eagle Gate, 2001), 10; Nolan P. Olsen,* Logan Temple: The First 100 Years

(Logan, Utah: Watkins and Sons, 1978), 73.

5. d. She purchased a member's temple recommend for $1

Just as the Lord protected the workers as they built the temple, he protected the completed temple from the desecration and abuse of those who would harm the structure or enter in unworthily. One such example of divine intervention took place at the dedication of the temple in May 1884. As President John Taylor watched the large numbers of people enter the temple, he suddenly turned to President Charles O. Card and said that a certain woman coming through the doorway was not worthy to enter the temple. It was discovered that this woman was not a member, and she was asked to leave. She had purchased the recommend from a member for a dollar. President Taylor had never seen this woman before, but the Spirit had whispered that of all the people in attendance, she was not worthy to be there.

Nolan P. Olsen, Logan Temple: The First 100 Years *(Logan, Utah: Watkins and Sons, 1978), 152–53.*

6. a. The decorative tablets on the west and east ends of the temple

President Heber C. Kimball prophesied the following in 1854 when referring to the Manti Temple: "The rock will be quarried from that hill to build it with and some of the stone from that quarry will be taken to help complete the Salt Lake Temple." This was literally fulfilled as the decorative tablets on both the west and east ends of the Salt Lake Temple are constructed of rock quarried from the Manti Temple quarry.

"Spiritual Manifestations in the Manti Temple," Millennial Star, *13 August 1888, 521.*

7. c. 1867

The Salt Lake Temple foundation was originally constructed of red sandstone. It was this foundation that was found to be cracked when uncovered after the Utah War. Due to the fact that the Saints had to rip the old foundation out and replace it with much stronger granite, the walls of the temple did not actually hit ground level until 1867, a good fourteen years after the cornerstone had been laid.

Chad S. Hawkins, The First 100 Temples *(Salt Lake City: Eagle Gate, 2001), 16.*

DAN BARKER

8. a. The Bowery on the temple lot

In 1850 the Salt Lake Musical and Dramatic Association was formed in Salt Lake City for the purpose of promoting drama and encouraging music. The association included the old Nauvoo Brass Band and the members of the dramatic club. In 1850 this was located on Temple Square, the Bowery, where the people met for worship on the Sabbath Day. The place was a general meetinghouse for civic gatherings as well as for religious meetings, and it also became the first theater. Here, in the early part of the year, "Robert Macaire" was played to crowded houses, and upon one occasion a number of Ute Indians witnessed the play.

Chronicles of Courage, Daughters of Utah Pioneers *(Salt Lake City; Utah Printing Company, 1990) 1:176.*

9. c. At the temple dedication, in which he told the Saints he wasn't satisfied with their efforts yet

Brigham Young said, "I might ask you if you are satisfied with what we have done today. I can say that I am not half satisfied and do not expect to be satisfied until I have whipped and driven the devils from off this earth," striking the top of the stand with his walking stick, making an impression of two knots and the way the stick in the stand. "There," he said, "I have marked the stand. Never mind, let those marks remain," which marks he felt should remain as a testimony of the earnestness with which he made the remark.

L. John Nuttall Diary Excerpts, *Ogden Kraut, ed. (Salt Lake City; Pioneer Press, 1994), 9.*

10. a. Heavenly

"1846, January 4. Since the death of Joseph and Hyrum, the building of the [Nauvoo] temple has gone on rapidly and contrary to the expectation and prophecy of Sidney Rigdon and others. The roof has been put on, the spire put up and beautifully ornamented. The temple is indeed a noble structure, and I suppose the architects of our day know not of what order to call it, Gothic, Doric, Corinthian or what. I call it heavenly."

Joseph Fielding, Diary (1843–46), Church Archives in "They Might Have Known That He Was Not a Fallen Prophet—The Nauvoo Journal of Joseph Fielding," transcribed and edited by Andrew F. Ehat, BYU Studies 19 (Winter 1979).

CATCH ALL

1. How much money was the recorder of licenses and blessings to receive per one hundred words?
   a. One cent
   b. Five cents
   c. Ten cents
   d. Two cents

2. What was seen in the night sky by future members of the Church, Heber C. Kimball and John P. Greene, the night Joseph Smith received the plates from the angel Moroni?
   a. An army marching to battle
   b. A heavenly choir
   c. The moon as bright as the sun
   d. The night as light as noon day

3. Porter Rockwell was found not guilty of the attempted assassination of ex-Governor Boggs, nevertheless what charge was he found guilty on?
   a. Treason
   b. Theft
   c. Jailbreak
   d. Debt

4. True or false? In the early years of the Church in the Salt Lake Valley, famous actors from the United States and England came to perform at the Salt Lake Theater.

5. How much did it cost to send a one-page letter over four hundred miles during the Nauvoo period of the Church?
   a. 2 cents
   b. 25 cents
   c. 10 cents
   d. 3 cents

6. Once the Pony Express was established in 1859–60, what was the cost per ounce for a letter?
   a. 50 cents
   b. $1
   c. $5
   d. 75 cents

7. Why did the Church call the majority of the brethren home in 1841?
   a. To speed up work on the Nauvoo Temple
   b. To use as manpower to dam the Mississippi River at Keokuk, Iowa
   c. They needed more LDS votes to get the right politicians in power
   d. War was threatened between the United States and England

8. When Joseph Smith read the Word of Wisdom to the School of the Prophets, how many used tobacco?
   a. 20 out of 21
   b. 11 out of 35
   c. 1 out of 25
   d. 25 out of 25

9. When Zion's camp returned to Kirtland, Dennis Lake, one of the members of the camp, did what to the Prophet?
   a. Thanked him for the experience
   b. Invited Joseph and his family over to dinner
   c. Apostatized and sued the Prophet
   d. Stole from the Prophet what he figured he was owed

10. True or false? During the early years of the Church, it was boys and young men that held the Aaronic Priesthood.

11. How much gold leaf does it take to cover a seven-foot angel Moroni statue?
    a. 16 oz.
    b. 1.5 oz.
    c. 24 oz.
    d. 5 oz.

12. When the Beehive organization began in 1913, what was one of the challenges issued to the girls?
    a. Hold your breath underwater for 1 minute
    b. Sleep with the bedroom window fully open for one night
    c. Read the Book of Mormon in one year
    d. Bring an investigator to Beehives at least once in the two-year program

ANSWERS

1. c. Ten cents

This was in a day when the average man worked for about fifty cents in a day. "At a conference in Kirtland the following was resolved, that the recorder of licenses and patriarchal blessings receive, for each one hundred words, ten cents."

Joseph Smith Jr., History of the Church *(Salt Lake City: Deseret Book, 1950), 2:528.*

2. a. An army marching to battle

The night that Joseph Smith received the plates from the angel Moroni, September 21, 1827, the heavens were alive with a panorama that caused many to take note. The Knights and Kimballs, who had never heard of Joseph Smith, took note of the night sky. Heber C. Kimball records the following in his journal:

I had retired to bed, when John P. Greene . . . who was living within a hundred steps of my house, came and waked me up, calling upon me to come out and behold the scenery in the heavens. I woke up and called my wife and Sister Fanny Young . . . who was living with us, and we went out-of-doors.

It was one of the most beautiful starlight nights, so clear that we could see to pick up a pin. We looked to the eastern horizon, and beheld a white smoke arise toward the heavens; as it ascended, it formed itself into a belt, and made a noise like the sound of the mighty wind, and continued southwest, forming a regular bow dipping in the western horizon. After the bow had formed, it began to widen out and grow clear and transparent, . . . it grew wide enough to contain twelve men abreast.

In this bow an army moved, commencing from the east and marching to the west; they continued marching until they reached the western horizon. They moved in platoons, and walked so close that the rear ranks trod in the steps of their file leaders, until the whole bow was literally crowded with soldiers. We could distinctly see the muskets, bayonets and knapsacks of the men, who wore caps and feathers like those used by the American soldiers in the last war with Britain; and also saw their officers with their swords and equipage, and the clashing and jingling of their implements of war, and could discover the forms and features of the men. The most profound order existed throughout the entire army; when the foremost man stepped every man stepped at the same time; I could hear the steps. When the front rank reached the western horizon a battle ensued, as we could distinctly hear the report of arms and the rush.

No man could judge of my feelings when I beheld that army of men, as plenty as ever I saw armies of men in the flesh; it seemed as though every hair of my head was alive.

This scenery we gazed upon for hours, until it began to disappear.

After I became acquainted with Mormonism, I learned that this took place the same evening that Joseph Smith received the records of the Book of Mormon from the angel Moroni who has held those records in this possession. My wife, being frightened at what she saw said, "Father Young, what does all this mean?" "Why it's one of the signs of the coming of the Son to Man," he replied, in a lively, pleased manner.

Orson F. Whitney, The Life of Heber C. Kimball *(Salt Lake City: Bookcraft, 1945), 15–17.*

3. c. Jailbreak

After his trial for the attempted assassination of Missouri's ex-Governor Lilburn W. Boggs, Porter Rockwell was found not guilty by the jury. Nevertheless, the same jury found him guilty of jailbreak. The judge sentenced him to five minutes in jail.

The Church News, *November 10, 1962.*

4. True

The theater was managed by Hyrum B. Clawson and John T. Caine, and during their years of management there appeared some of the noted actors of England and America. The local members of the dramatic association played without remuneration, but those who were brought from the eastern states were given good compensation, for it was a long journey over the Plains from the Missouri River by stagecoach to Utah. Among these were Thomas S. Lyne, Sir George Pauncefort, John McCullough, Julia Dean Hayne, Annie Adams, and Sarah Alexander. In 1867, C. W. Couldock came with his daughter from Rawlins, Wyoming, by stage coach.

Chronicles of Courage, Daughters of Utah Pioneers *(Salt Lake City: Utah Printing Company, 1990) 1:180.*

5. b. 25 cents

Between 1816 and 1845 the cost for sending a single sheet letter less than thirty miles was six cents; not over 80 miles, ten cents; not over 150 miles, 12½ cents; and not over 400 miles, 18¾ cents. Greater distances cost 25 cents. Letters of two or more sheets required additional postage in proportion. If a letter weighed more than an ounce, the postage quadrupled. For many, postal communication was a luxury. Prior to 1847 when postage stamps were authorized, the collection of postage from the addressee had led to many abuses, including the payment by the addressee of letters containing offensive and insulting messages.

Arthur E. Summerfield, U.S. Mail: The Story of the United States Postal Service *(New York: Holt, Rinehart and Winston, 1960), 45–46; see also Clyde Kelly,* United States Postal Policy *(New York and London: D. Appleton and Co., 1932), 57–58.*

6. c. $5

The Pony Express was organized in 1859–60 making huge

improvements timewise on the speed of the mail, but not cost. The Express drivers were expected to do three laps between stations (usually twenty-four miles apart) at an average of 8 miles an hour. At this rate, a letter from New York to San Francisco could arrive in 13 days. In fact George A. Smith wrote in April of 1861: "The Pony Express proved to be quite an institution. The news of the surrender of Fort Sumter reached here (Salt Lake City) in seven days."

Not to be sarcastic, but I believe that pretty much rivals with today, and to think it's all done by plane.

What was the cost per ounce for a letter on the Pony Express System? Five dollars! Ouch!

Letter to John L. Smith from Brigham Young, History of Brigham Young, *Ms. 1858. (1844–77) Church Historian's Library, Salt Lake City., 165; William Edwin Berrett,* The Restored Church *(Salt Lake City: Deseret Book, 1973), 310.*

7. d. War was threatened between the United States and England

"In 1841, a threat of war between the United States and England caused the majority of the brethren to be called home to Nauvoo."

William Edwin Berrett, The Restored Church *(Salt Lake City: Deseret Book, 1973), 153.*

8. a. 20 out of 21

"When the Word of Wisdom [D&C 89] was first presented by the Prophet Joseph (as he came out of the translating room) and was read to the School, there were twenty out of the twenty-one who used tobacco and they all immediately threw their tobacco and pies into the fire."

Remarks of Zebedee Coltrin on Kirtland, Ohio, History of the Church, Minutes, Salt Lake City School of the Prophets, October 3, 1883.

9. c. Apostatized and sued the Prophet

"The next spring most of the Elders were called to volunteer to go and redeem Jackson County. Albert Miner told Mr. Dennis Lake he would draw cuts, to see who would go and who would stay and take care of both families. It fell on Albert Miner to stay and take care of the families. Dennis Lake went with the company to redeem Jackson County and when he got back he apostatized and sued Joseph Smith for three months work, $60.00."

Autobiography of Tamma Durfee, Typescript, HBLL; http://www.boap.org/

10. False

During the years 1829–45 the Aaronic Priesthood was composed primarily of adults with the exception of a few outstanding youth. Their primary duty was to visit members in their homes. Their quorums were stake quorums. This situation resulted primarily from the fact that the endowment ceremony was not in place yet and therefore fewer men were called to the Melchizedek Priesthood.

From the years 1846–77 more men held the Melchizedek Priesthood since one had to be an elder to have their endowment, but men were also called to serve in acting positions in the Aaronic Priesthood. During this time period very few young men held the Aaronic Priesthood.

In 1877 the First Presidency instructed that every worthy young man receive priesthood ordination. Soon boys from ages 11 to 18 received the priesthood; most became deacons and stayed such until becoming elders. Few boys blessed or passed the sacrament or did what is now called home teaching.

In 1908 the First Presidency restructured the Aaronic Priesthood to be a priesthood for boys. They approved that worthy boys be ordained at set ages and advance through each office: deacons at age 12, teachers at 15, priests at 18, and elders at 21. . . .

In 1928 the ages of 12, 15, and 18 were changed to 12, 15, 17, respectively, with the elders' age set at 20. That age was reduced to 18 in October 1934, but by December it was raised to 19. In 1954 the teachers' age became 14, and the priest's age was changed to 16, so the ages became 12, 14, and 16, and elders were ordained at age 20 (now 18).

Arnold K. Garr, Donald Q. Cannon, and Richard O. Cowan, Encyclopedia of Latter-day Saint History *(Salt Lake City: Deseret Book, 2000), 1–2.*

11. b. 1.5 oz.

"The total weight of gold leaf required to cover a seven-foot statue of the angel Moroni is 1.5 ounces."

Chad S. Hawkins, The First 100 Temples *(Salt Lake City: Eagle Gate, 2001), 274.*

12. b. Sleep with the bedroom window fully open for one night

"The Beehive class, a program developed for young women ages 12 to 13, was organized in 1913 to replace the Junior Class in the

Young Lady's Mutual Improvement Association. Established guidelines required the "Young ladies" to accomplish goals to 'sleep outside or with wide open window; refrain from candy, chewing gum, sundaes, and sodas for at least two months; and, know the proper use of hot and cold baths.'"

Arnold K. Garr, Donald Q. Cannon, and Richard O. Cowan, Encyclopedia of Latter-day Saint History *(Salt Lake City: Deseret Book, 2000), 80.*

EDUCATION

1. Who is considered the Father of Adult Education in America?
   a. Professor Charles Anton
   b. Benjamin Franklin
   c. Joseph Smith Jr.
   d. Karl G. Maeser

2. The University of the State of Deseret (1850) was also known as what?
   a. The Parents School
   b. The Siblings School
   c. The University of Utah
   d. The Latter-day Saint Business College

3. How old was Caroline Davis when she started to teach school during the Missouri years of the Church?
   a. 19
   b. 21
   c. 13
   d. 15

4. How many days of formal education did Brigham Young have?
   a. 11 days
   b. 365 days
   c. 43 days
   d. 571 days

5. How old was Brigham Young's daughter Susa Young Gates when she entered the University of Deseret (forerunner to the University of Utah)?
   a. 12 years
   b. 17 years
   c. 13 years
   d. 16 years

Answers

1. c. Joseph Smith Jr.

The Prophet Joseph Smith started up the School of the Prophets in Kirtland, Ohio, which was the first organized school for adult education in America. This school was to instruct the brethren in the gospel and academics. The school was put on hold when the Saints left Nauvoo. More than twenty years later, Brigham Young reorganized the School of the Prophets in 1867. Again, academics and spiritual classes were stressed in addition to activities such as raising funds for the Perpetual Emigration Fund, instituting a mercantile boycott of merchants who opposed the Church, establishing the Provo Woolen Mills, reducing wages for Utah workers to make the prices of Utah manufactured goods more competitive with goods that would now be shipped from the East, and finally promoting the construction of the railroad from Salt Lake City to Ogden.

Leonard J. Arrington, Great Basin Kingdom: An Economic History of the Latter-day Saints, 1830–1900 *(Cambridge: Harvard University Press), 245–51.*

2. a. The Parents School

"In 1850, the University of the State of Deseret (the forerunner to the University of Utah) was commonly known as the Parents School and was held in the parlor of John Pack's home. Dr. Collins taught and tuition was eight dollars per quarter. Since money was scarce, food could be used to pay for school."

Clarissa Young Spencer and Mable Harmer, Brigham Young at Home *(Salt Lake City: Deseret Book, 1947), 132.*

3. c. 13

"I was very sick with chills and fever. I was immediately healed after being baptized and confirmed. I was thirteen years old in October before I taught school the next following summer. I had about 25 pupils. I learned them what was taught in common schools, the girls to knit and sew. This was in Missouri."

Autobiography of Caroline Frances Angell Davis Holbrook, http://www.boap.org/

4. a. 11 days

As a youth, Brigham Young attended only eleven days of formal schooling. He later said:

> Brother Heber and I never went to school until we got into Mormonism. That was the first of our schooling. We never had the opportunity of letters in our youth, but we had the privilege of picking up brush, chopping down trees, rolling log and working amongst the roots, and of getting our shins, feet and toes bruised. I learned how to make bread, wash the dishes, milk the cows and make butter; and can beat most of the women in this community at housekeeping. Those are about all the advantages I gained in my youth. I know how to economize, for my father had to do it.

Journal of Discourses, *26 vols. (Salt Lake City: Deseret Book, 1974),* *5:97.*

5. c. 13 years

Susa Young Gates, daughter of Brigham Young, was attending the University of Deseret (the forerunner to the University of Utah) at the ripe old age of thirteen.

Carolyn W. D. Person, "Susa Young Gates," in Mormon Sisters, *Bushman, ed, 201–23; Rebecca Foster Cornwall, "Susa Y. Gates," in* Sister Saints, *Burgess-Olsen ed., 63–93.*

FIRSTS

1. When was the first Thanksgiving feast celebrated in the Salt Lake Valley?
    a. August 1848
    b. November 1847
    c. November 1848
    d. December 1847

2. When was the first Medal of Honor awarded to a private in the US army (by the way, the recipient was LDS)?
    a. During the Blackhawk War
    b. During the Korean War
    c. During the Civil War
    d. During the 1st World War

3. In which running event did a Latter-day Saint first set a world record?
    a. The 5,000
    b. The 220
    c. The marathon
    d. The 100

4. Who developed the first Egyptian grammar book in America?
    a. Professor Charles Anthon
    b. Joseph Smith
    c. Orson Hyde
    d. John Murdock

5. Which LDS man became California's first millionaire?
   a. Levi Hancock
   b. Willard Richards
   c. Samuel Brannan
   d. Samuel Chambers

6. Where was the first mercantile store set up in Salt Lake City?
   a. At Sugarhouse
   b. In the same house where the Parent School (forerunner to the University of Utah) was located
   c. The Lion House
   d. At the tithing yards across from the Salt Lake Temple

7. What was the theme of the first-ever painting of a Book of Mormon scene?
   a. The Baptism of Limhi
   b. Nephi and his brothers building the ship
   c. Ammon defending the flocks of the king
   d. Christ's visit to the Americas

8. What was Daniel Garn's occupation before he became Utah's first territorial prison warden?
   a. A teacher
   b. A lawyer
   c. A General Authority
   d. A prisoner

9. Which of these world records was set by a Latter-day Saint first?
   a. The high jump
   b. The number of children in a family
   c. The marathon
   d. The longest beard

10. When was the first attempt at illustrating the Book of Mormon?
    a. 1829
    b. 1830
    c. 1888
    d. 1912

Answers

1.   a. August 1848
"The first Thanksgiving Dinner of the Saints in the Salt Lake Valley was on August 10, 1848 to celebrate a bounteous harvest. Interestingly, a second Thanksgiving Dinner was celebrated just days prior to the October General Conference the same year. This celebration was for the safe return of the Mormon Battalion."
The Church News, *November 24, 1948*

2.   d. During the 1st World War
"February 9, 1919: The U.S. Congress awards Private Thomas C. Neibur the Medal of Honor, making him the first Latter-day Saint and the first private in the U.S. Army to receive the award."
Richard Neitzel Holzapfel et al., On This Day in the Church *(Salt Lake City: Eagle Gate, 2000), 30.*

Here's a little more information on the story: "In May of 1898, Thomas C. Neibaur, later a World War I army private awarded the U.S. Congressional Medal of Honor for defending fellow soldiers from attack and taking eleven enemy soldiers as prisoners, all after being wounded in battle, [was] born in Sharon, Idaho."
Richard Neitzel Holzapfel et al., On This Day in the Church *(Salt Lake City: Eagle Gate, 2000), 98.*

3.   b. The 220
"The first running world record set by a Latter-day Saint [was] set by Creed Haymond in 1919 during the 220-yard dash. His time was 21.0 seconds. This time stood until Jesse Owen broke the record at the 1936 Olympics."
The Church News, *June 19, 1999.*

4.   b. Joseph Smith
"In Kirtland, Joseph Smith [developed] the first Egyptian grammar book in America. This was never published and most likely used only by the Prophet Joseph Smith."
William Edwin Berrett, The Restored Church *(Salt Lake City: Deseret Book, 1973), 99.*

5. c. Samuel Brannan

Samuel Brannan was an energetic Elder for the Church in the New York City area. He is the individual who chartered the ship "Brooklyn" to transport 238 Saints to California. He became California's first millionaire, although [he] lost his fortune through unwise business investments and lived the last few years of his life in poverty. This wealth was obtained through fraud. Pretending to be Brigham Young's representative in California, he stole the Church's tithing for a period of time before he was caught.

William Edwin Berrett, The Restored Church *(Salt Lake City: Deseret Book, 1973), 231; Richard S. Van Wagoner and Steven C. Walker,* A Book of Mormons *(Salt Lake City: Signature Books, 1982), 22.*

6. b. In the same house where the Parent School (forerunner to the University of Utah) was located

The first mercantile store in the Salt Lake Valley was established in the home of John and Julia Pack in the year 1850. It was in a room across from the parlor where the first university classes were in session (forerunner to the University of Utah).

Clarissa Young Spencer and Mable Harmer, Brigham Young at Home *(Salt Lake City: Deseret Book, 1947), 132.*

7. a. The Baptism of Limhi

"George M. Ottinger painted the Baptism of Limhi, which was a scene depicting Alma the Elder baptizing at the Waters of Mormon. He painted this picture in 1872 and [it] measures a very huge seven and a half feet by five feet."

Noel A. Carmack, "A Picturesque and Dramatic History," BYU Studies, *Vol. 47, no. 2 (2008), 115.*

8. d. A prisoner

It's interesting to note that the first territorial prison warden in Utah was actually a prisoner first. Daniel Garn was imprisoned in Richmond, Missouri, during the dark Missouri years of the Church. His crime? Being a Mormon.

The Church News, *August 19, 1967*

9. a. The high jump

"In 1917, Clint Larsen set a world record high jump of 6 feet 3 inches. This [was] the first time a Latter-day Saint [had] set a world record."

Paul B. Skousen, The Skousen Book of Mormon World Records *(Springville, Utah: Cedar Fort, 2004), 376.*

10. c. 1888

"The first attempt at illustrating the Book of Mormon was in 1888, with the publication of *The Story of the Book of Mormon* by George Reynolds."

Noel A. Carmack, "A Picturesque and Dramatic History," BYU Studies, Vol. 47, no. 2 (2008), 115.

GOVERNMENT AND THE CHURCH

1. The Mormon Battalion of 1846 was not the first time the government solicited the Church for men. In 1837 the government approached the Church for help with what?
   a. To restore property back to the Church that had been lost in Jackson County, Missouri
   b. To round up all the British loyal to England and send them back home
   c. To put down a Seminole uprising
   d. To prepare to invade South Carolina if they did not give up their slaves

2. Who was the next prophet to visit the President of the United States after Joseph Smith visited Martin Van Buren?
   a. John Taylor
   b. Heber J. Grant
   c. Lorenzo Snow
   d. Joseph F. Smith

3. Who was the first US President to speak in the tabernacle?
   a. Theodore Roosevelt
   b. Abraham Lincoln
   c. Ulysses S. Grant
   d. Grover Cleveland

4. Who is the only US President to utter the phrase "Mormon Church" in his inaugural speech?
   a. Woodrow Wilson
   b. Abraham Lincoln
   c. James A. Garfield
   d. James K. Polk

5. After the Missouri persecutions, Sidney Rigdon drummed up much feeling to have the government do what to the state of Missouri?
   a. Oust them from the Union of States
   b. Force them to become a free state
   c. Give the land back to the natives
   d. Make the citizens of Jackson County pay capital gains tax on the land taken from the Saints

6. Who is the only US President to be mentioned in a temple dedication prayer?
   a. Theodore Roosevelt
   b. William Howard Taft
   c. Woodrow Wilson
   d. Warren G. Harding

7. Which US President was the first to appoint a Latter-day Saint to a subcabinet position?
   a. John Tyler
   b. Zachary Taylor
   c. Benjamin Harrison
   d. Woodrow Wilson

8. When Stephen A. Douglas attacked the Church in speeches from 1857–60, which US President backed the Church?
   a. Millard Fillmore
   b. Franklin Pierce
   c. Abraham Lincoln
   d. James Buchanan

ANSWERS

1. c. To put down a Seminole uprising

The Mormon Battalion of 1846 is not the first time that the government has asked the Mormons to supply men in a cause. In October of 1837, Edward Partridge wrote a letter to his brother stating that the government required 1000 natives and approximately 150 to 200 white men to help put down the Seminoles in Florida. Only a few of the Saints responded to this call from the government.

Warren A. Jennings, "What Crime Have I Been Guilty of?" BYU Studies, *Summer 1978, 521–22.*

John P. Greene comments on the above situation (the government asking for troops in October of 1837) and states that many volunteers came forward. He says:

> "And here we wish particularly to call attention to the fact, that the Mormons in Caldwell were the regular state militia for that county, and were at this time acting under the legal authorities of the county. To prove that they were distinctly regarded by the executive as the state militia, we relate the fact, that, sometime in September last, Gen. Parks being ordered to collect a body of troops out of his brigade, which should be ready to march to the frontier in case of aggression from Indians, called for a company of 60 men from Caldwell County; whereupon, 300 volunteers, (all Mormons,) presented themselves, from whom he selected his company of minutemen."

John P. Greene, Facts Relative to the Expulsion of the Mormons or Latter-day Saints, From the State of Missouri, Under the Exterminating Order *(Cincinnati: R. P. Brooks, 1839).*

2. d. Joseph F. Smith

President Taft visited Utah six times, breaking the record for presidential visits to Utah. He also had the prophet at the time, Joseph F. Smith, visit him at the White House. This made Joseph F. Smith the first prophet to visit the White House since Joseph Smith called on Van Buren. Taft also invited the Tabernacle Choir to perform at the White House as a gesture of goodwill. Around this time prominent Mormon politicians like Reed Smoot and J. Reuben Clark were also called on to help build the Church's reputation with the President.

Michael K. Winder, Presidents and Prophets *(American Fork, Utah: Covenant, 2007), 211.*

3. a. Theodore Roosevelt
"Teddy Roosevelt visits Utah and becomes the first US President to speak in the Tabernacle."
Michael K. Winder, Presidents and Prophets *(American Fork, Utah: Covenant, 2007), 184.*

4. c. James A. Garfield
"James A. Garfield is sworn into office and becomes the only President to utter the phrase 'Mormon Church' in an inaugural address."
Michael K. Winder, Presidents and Prophets *(American Fork, Utah: Covenant, 2007), 143.*

5. a. Oust them from the Union of States
"It is doubtful if Joseph Smith, after the expulsion from Missouri, seriously expected to be reinstated in that land at that time or even to receive compensation for the losses incurred. That hope had not died out, however, among the Saints. Sidney Rigdon even proposed a scheme to oust Missouri from the Union of States and worked up considerable feeling over it."
William Edwin Berrett, The Restored Church *(Salt Lake City: Deseret Book, 1973), 164.*

6. c. Woodrow Wilson
"Having just suffered a major stroke, Woodrow Wilson becomes the only President blessed by name in a temple dedicatory prayer. In Hawaii, President Heber J. Grant prays, 'We pray Thee to bless Woodrow Wilson, the president of these United States. Touch him with the healing power of Thy Holy Spirit and make him whole. We pray that his life may be precious in Thy sight, and may the inspiration that comes from Thee ever abide with him.'"
N.B. Lundwall, Temples of the Most High *(Salt Lake City: Bookcraft, 1962), 148.*

7. d. Woodrow Wilson
"In September of 1917, U.S. president Woodrow Wilson appoints James H. Moyle, the first Latter-day Saint to serve in a subcabinet position in the United States, as assistant secretary of the U.S. Treasury."

Richard Neitzel Holzapfel et al., On This Day in the Church *(Salt Lake City: Eagle Gate, 2000), 183.*

8. c. Abraham Lincoln

"When Stephen A. Douglas spoke out against the Church in speeches from 1857 to 1860, Lincoln responded by pointing out the inconsistency between Douglas's idea of popular sovereignty and his denunciation of the Mormons as 'alien enemies and outlaws.' Lincoln also saw Douglas's advocating the repeal of Utah's territorial status as a way of trying to destroy Mormonism."

George U. Hubbard, "Abraham Lincoln as Seen by the Mormons," Utah Historical Quarterly *31 (Spring 1963), 91–108.*

Meetings

1. The first general conference to take place on a river boat happened where?
   a. On the Mississippi River at Nauvoo, Illinois
   b. On the Missouri River at Winter Quarters, Nebraska
   c. On the Big Blue River at Jackson County, Missouri
   d. On Lake Erie near Fairport, Ohio (just north of Kirtland, Ohio)

2. What big event happened during the April 1844 General Conference?
   a. Joseph Smith was nominated to the presidency of the United States
   b. Joseph Smith was officially recognized as President of the Church of Jesus Christ of Latter-day Saints
   c. It was voted to destroy the *Nauvoo Expositor*
   d. It was agreed to send an expedition to the Great Basin

3. During the 1800s, home teachers were referred to as what?
   a. Visiting or home teachers
   b. Acting or block teachers
   c. Home or family teachers
   d. Ward or branch teachers

4. In Tamma Durfee's autobiography, she writes that she heard the Prophet Joseph Smith preach for how long during a meeting in Kirtland?
   a. 1 hour
   b. 3 hours
   c. 5 hours
   d. 6½ hours

5. What year was the Sunday School organized?
   a. 1830
   b. 1839
   c. 1903
   d. 1867

6. True or false? Only gospel topics were taught during Sunday school meetings.

ANSWERS

1.   c. On the Big Blue River at Jackson County, Missouri

"The first general conference held on a river boat occurred in April of 1833. This meeting was held on the Big Blue River in Jackson County, Missouri."

Paul B. Skousen, The Skousen Book of Mormon World Records (Springville, Utah: Cedar Fort, 2004), 271.

2.   a. Joseph Smith was nominated to the presidency of the United States

"During the April 1844 General Conference of the Church, Joseph Smith was officially nominated for President of the United States."

Paul B. Skousen, The Skousen Book of Mormon World Records (Springville, Utah: Cedar Fort, 2004), 272.

3.   b. Acting or block teachers

"During the nineteenth century, home teachers were referred to as teachers, acting teachers, or block teachers. In 1908 they became ward teachers, and it wasn't until the 1960s that they became home teachers. What's interesting is that teachers, priests, or Melchizedek Priesthood holders were called with the assistance of the deacons."

Rex A. Anderson, "A Documentary History of the Lord's Way of Watching over the Church by the Priesthood through the Ages." Master's thesis, Brigham Young University, 1974; Gary L. Phelps, "Home Teaching—Attempts by the Latter-day Saints to Establish an Effective Program during the Nineteenth Century." Master's thesis, Brigham Young University, 1975.

Side note to question 3: I seriously doubt the Church keeps a record of the farthest distance walked to a home teaching visit. However, if they did, I think my parents, George and Marion Barker of the Banff, Alberta Branch of the Calgary West Stake just might hold the record. They live high up in the Canadian Rockies, and the people that attend their branch are sprinkled out over the towns of Canmore, Exshaw, Lake Louise, and Banff and at various tourist hotspots in Banff National Park. My parents have been assigned as home and visiting teachers to as many as eight individuals in a month, taking them as far away as a one-hundred-and-eighty-mile round trip to Saskatchewan Crossing. One of the people they visit is a young lady that works at the Lake O'Hara

Lodge in the Park. To keep this area pristine, the park only allows two buses in each day. It's necessary to book the bus in advance to take the ride in. My parents hoped that someone would not show up and that they could get a place on the bus. But the bus was full, so there was no way they could get on. Not letting a full bus get in the way of their visit to this young lady, my parents decided to hike into the lodge. Instead of taking the shorter route, which is a seven-mile trip on the road, they chose instead to take the ten-mile scenic hike through the forest. When my parents, both well into their sixties at the time, showed up for the visit, this young lady was amazed that they would do this for her and spoke often of this act of love in church.

4. c. 5 hours

"I heard Joseph once talk and preach for five hours to a congregation, and no one was tired. This was in Kirtland before they built the first temple."

Autobiography of Tamma Durfee, Typescript, HBLL; http://www. boap.org/

5. d. 1867

Utah's non-Mormons in fact were partly responsible for reviving the ward's appetite for meetings. The problem came not so much from the unsavory Gentile, but from "those of Educated and refined manners [who] are able to exercise great influence." These, with the children of "apostates and traitors."

To defuse this new Gentile threat, church leaders turned to the Thirteenth Ward. Brigham Young, George A. Smith, Daniel H. Wells, George Q. Canon, and other prominent churchmen met with ward officers on 30 March 1867 and resolved to form a Sunday school. During the organizational spate of the 1850s, several congregations had begun short-lived Sabbath schools, and the middle 1860s brought several more. But Woolley's (Bishop Woolley) proposed school was the first since the city's bishops had agreed, in a major policy decision, to counter the denominational academies with LDS Sabbath schools. Woolley had moved with untypical dispatch—probably at the nudging of his priesthood leaders, who hoped to make the Thirteenth Ward's school an example for other wards to follow.

The project began impressively. On 7 April 1867 leading churchmen George A. Smith and George Q. Cannon called a "large assembly of children" to order and named A. Milton Musser as superintendent. Also present was Bishop Woolley, most ward officers, and even Mormondom's "first lady" Eliza R. Snow, who penned for the occasion a poem, "In Our Lovely Deseret." The succeeding weeks were as notable. The school soon acquired a library of 150 books and, more importantly, the services of such leading LDS intellectuals as William S. Godbe, William H. Shearman, E.L.T. Harrison, and Eli Kelsey. In addition, Mormon General Authorities Ezra T. Benson, Orson Hyde, George A. Smith, and President Brigham Young himself periodically taught the "scholars." Such talent quickly attracted an average attendance of over two hundred youth and produced a model that other wards copied. Before a year had expired, President Young was acknowledging "the happy results arising from our Sabbath schools."

Minutes of the Bishops' Meetings, 30 November 1865 and 7 March 1867, Presiding Bishopric Papers; Thomas Edgar Lyon, "Evangelical Protestant Missionary Activities in Mormon Dominated Areas," (PhD diss., University of Utah, 1962); Thirteenth Ward General Minutes, 30 March 1867; "Minutes of the Thirteenth Ward Sunday School Jubilee," Thirteenth Ward Teachers' Report Meetings, 1891–1907, 17 December 1899, LDS Archives; Earlier Schools: Seventeenth Ward Bishop's Record, January 1854, p. 51, LDS Archives; Arrington, From Quaker to Latter-day Saint: Bishop Edwin D. Woolley *(Salt Lake City, Deseret Book, 1976), 459; Minutes of the Bishops' Meetings, 8 March 1866 and 7 March 1867. Sabbath School Decision: ibid., 7 March 1867;* New Views of Mormon History, *Davis Bitton and Maureen Ursenbach Beecher, eds. (Salt Lake City, University of Utah Press, 1987), 149–50.*

6. False

"At first, without didactic teaching materials, some wards taught academic subjects during Sunday school such as astronomy."

New Views on Mormon History, *Davis Bitton and Maureen Usenbach Beecher, eds. (Salt Lake City, University of Utah Press, 1987), 150.*

MISSIONS

1. What did Jacob Hamblin do to provide for his way back home to Nauvoo at the completion of his mission?
   a. Gave a much-needed blessing
   b. Sang hymns for money
   c. Sold copies of the Book of Mormon
   d. Gave harmonica lessons

2. After the last member left the Palmyra-Manchester area for Kirtland, Ohio, in 1831, how many years was it before a member family returned to the area?
   a. 27 years
   b. 93 years
   c. 84 years
   d. 52 years

3. How did Spencer W. Kimball learn that he was to serve a mission?
   a. His dad made an announcement over the podium at his high school graduation
   b. He got a letter from the First Presidency, calling him to a mission
   c. He had a dream
   d. It was stated in his patriarchal blessing

4. Other than during war times, in which year were the fewest missionaries sent out by the Church and why were so few sent?
   a. 1833, due to construction of the Kirtland Temple

b.   1857, because of the arrival of Johnston's Army in the Salt Lake Valley

c.   1852, because the Church was more concerned with the gathering of the Saints in the Salt Lake Valley

d.   1845, due to the hurried construction of the Nauvoo Temple

5.   Thomas Biesinger was called to serve in Czechoslovakia in 1883. After one month of preaching, he was thrown into jail. What happened to the man that made the accusation against Elder Biesinger?

a.   He became somewhat of a local hero for turning in a Mormon missionary

b.   He died a painful death

c.   He lost all that he possessed

d.   He was baptized

6.   In what year did the First Presidency announce that full-time missionaries were no longer required to pay tithing?

a.   1831

b.   1902

c.   1953

d.   1847

7.   For the most part, the Church experienced success among the Native American tribes; however, which tribe could not understand the principles of the gospel?

a.   The Sioux

b.   The Apache

c.   The Blackfoot

d.   The Cree of Canada

8.   Which individual served the most missions for the Church?

a.   Joseph Smith

b.   Samuel Smith

c.   Parley P. Pratt

d.   Orson Pratt

9.   True or false? Levi Hancock and Zebedee Coltrin baptized seventeen members of a mob that had threatened them the previous day.

Answers

1. a. Gave a much-needed blessing

This story is from the mission of Jacob Hamblin after he had received word to return home to Nauvoo subsequent to the death of Joseph and Hyrum.

> After, starting I began to reflect on my situation. I must travel on the river steamers from Pittsburgh to Nauvoo, via Cincinnati and St. Louis, and I had only two dollars in my pocket. I had been often surprised, when traveling on foot at the pains people would take to invite me to ride or to step into a grocery and take a lunch, and I had considerable faith that the Lord would soften the heart of someone to assist me, when I was in need.
>
> When I arrived in Pittsburgh, I had one dollar left. There were two steamers at the landing about to start for St. Louis. They offered to take passengers very cheap. I told the captain of one of them, that I would give all the money I had for a passage to St. Louis. He took my money and gave me a ticket, but appeared rather cross.
>
> I was soon on my way down the river, but still a long way from home, and without money or anything to eat. I began to feel the want of food.
>
> Nothing special occurred with me until evening, when the lamps were lit in the passenger's cabin. I was then asked by a young married lady, if I was not a "Mormon" Elder. I replied that I was; and she told me that her little child was dying with the scarlet fever, and she wished me to lay hands on it and heal it.
>
> I replied that I could administer to it, and I presumed that the Lord would heal it. I asked her if she believed in such things. She said that she did, and that she belonged to the Church, but her husband did not. I was puzzled in my mind to know what to do, for the boat was crowded with passengers, and all unbelievers excepting the mother of the sick child and myself. It seemed like a special providence that, just then the lamp in the cabin should fall from its hangings, and leave us all in the dark.
>
> Before another lamp could be lit, I had administered to the child, and rebuked the fever in the name of the Lord Jesus, unobserved by those around. The Lord blessed the administration, and the child was healed.
>
> The mother called her husband, and said to him, "Little Mary is healed; now do not say anything against 'Mormonism.'" The man

looked at his child, and said to me, "I am not a believer in any kind of religion, but I am on my way to Iowa, opposite to Nauvoo, where I presume you are going. You are welcome to board with me all the way, and if you want any money I will let you have it."

James A. Little, Jacob Hamblin in Three Mormon Classics, *Preston Nibley, comp. (Salt Lake City: Bookcraft, 1988), 211–12.*

2.   c. 84 years

Willard Bean, a former boxer from Utah, and Rebecca, his bride of less than a year, were sent in 1915 to take care of the farm (Joseph Smith Sr. farm) after the former owner moved. They were challenged to preach the gospel and make friends for the Church in that area. They became the first Latter-day Saints to live in Manchester in eighty-four years. Their call is equally as interesting. Brother Bean and Rebecca attended a conference in Richfield, Utah, presided over by President Joseph F. Smith. President Smith was looking for the right man to represent the Church and run the Joseph Smith farm in Manchester, New York. President Smith later said that when Willard walked in, "The impression was so strong—it was just like a voice said to me, 'There's your man.'"

Despite severe anti-Mormon prejudice, the Beans persevered and eventually won the respect of the people in the nearby village of Palmyra. Willard was instrumental in helping the church purchase several other important historical sites in the area. What was expected to be "five years or more" of service in Palmyra turned out to be twenty-five. When the Beans returned to Salt Lake City, they were grandparents.

"Willard Bean: Palmyra's Fighting Parson," Ensign, *June 1985, 26–27.*

3.   a. His dad made an announcement over the podium at his high school graduation

At his graduation ceremony, Spencer was stunned to hear his father announce over the podium that instead of going to college, Spencer would be serving a mission. He hadn't really given it much immediate thought, since most missionaries at that time were older men, but he embraced the formal call when it arrived from Salt Lake City. To finance his mission he sold his horse and spent the summer working at a dairy near Globe, Arizona. The eighteen-hour days were grueling, but at the end of the summer the cigar-smoking non-Mormon dairy owner threw a party for Spencer and gave him a gold watch to take on his mission.

"The Life and Ministry of Spencer W. Kimball," Teachings of Presidents of the Church: Spencer W. Kimball *(2006), xiv-xxxvii.*

4. c. 1852, because the Church was more concerned with the gathering of the Saints in the Salt Lake Valley

"During 1852 the Church made a concerted effort at having as many emigrants arrive in the Salt Lake Valley as possible. It's the year with the fewest missionaries, but also the year with the largest number of emigrants."

James A. Little, From Kirtland to Salt Lake City *(Salt Lake City, 1890) as quoted in Larsen,* Prelude to the Kingdom, *112.*

5. d. He was baptized

In 1883 German-born Thomas Biesinger, who was living in Lehi, Utah, received a call to serve in the European mission. He and Paul Hammer were sent to Prague, Czechoslovakia, then part of the Austro-Hungarian Empire. The missionaries were forbidden by law to proselyte and so initiated casual conversations with people they met. These conversations often turned to the subject of religion. After working in this way for only a month, Elder Biesinger was arrested and held in prison for two months. When he gained his freedom, he had the blessing of baptizing Antonin Just, whose accusation had led to this arrest. Brother Just became the first Latter-day Saint residing in Czechoslovakia.

Kahlile Mehr, "Enduring Believers: Czechoslovakia and the LDS Church, 1884–1990," Journal of Mormon History *(Fall 1992), 112–13;* Our Heritage *(Salt Lake City: The Church of Jesus Christ of Latter-day Saints, 1996), 95.*

6. b. 1902

"February 4, 1902: The First Presidency announces the policy that full-time missionaries need not pay tithing."

Richard Neitzel Holzapfel et al., On This Day in the Church *(Salt Lake City: Eagle Gate, 2000), 26.*

7. a. The Sioux

The following is a mission experience of John Lowe Butler, having been sent to the Sioux Indians on a mission by the Prophet Joseph Smith:

We had but little success among the Indians this time; they did not like us at all. They stole our horses and shot our cattle and came very near shooting us. We started our folks toward home, my family numbering my wife and five children. Well, as I say, we started them from home, and Brother Emmett and myself were to stay and find our horses. We stayed and found them, but the Indians took them from us again; then we had to fly for our lives. Now we started to go right between two lakes and the Indians tried to head us to waylay us and kill us. We had then not tasted one bit for eight or nine days. I prayed to the Lord to look down in mercy upon us and strengthen us and enable us to endure the trials and sufferings of hunger that we had to pass through. We got to the point between the lakes and headed them without interruption from the Indians. I could not tell the reason only that the Lord was our friend and changed the mind of the Indians so that they turned from their bloody design for they meant to kill us if they only could catch us.

After we had passed the point of the lakes, there was a stream of water running into the lake, running on our right hand and the spirit of the Lord told me that if I will turn aside and go down to the river I should find something to eat. I told Brother Emmett and we turned aside and went down to the stream. We had our rifles with us, but we had not seen any game at all; everything seemed to be far away when we wanted them close. Well, as we were going down, I had several thoughts come into my head; I could fancy seeing a fat deer standing on the bank of the stream, cooling this thirsty tongue. Then I thought I could see a good fat elk grazing on the bank of the stream, but we had gotten there and I could see no deer nor any elk. My mind was darkened, and I felt to murmur and called upon God and asked him why he had caused us to come so far out of our road and then not find anything to eat. I cast my eyes upon the stream, not knowing which way to go or what to do for we were weak and could hardly walk. I had not my eyes long in that direction when all of a sudden I saw thousands of fish in the water and fine large ones they were, too. I looked with wonder and astonishment and I thanked the Lord for his mercy and loving kindness unto us and I asked his forgiveness for doubting him and prayed for his holy spirit to enable me to put my trust in him more than I had hitherto done. We then caught fish and fed our hungry appetites, and then starting on our journey, thanked God for his watchfulness over us and his blessings unto us, and the Lord did continue to pour down his blessings upon us, so that he did deliver us from the bloodthirsty savages and enabled us to arrive home safely without any harm to ourselves.

We arrived about twelve miles from Nauvoo on the night of the fifth of October (1842?). I wanted to get to conference, it being the next day, so I got up the next morning and got on a horse and went to Nauvoo to conference, and I got there just as it commenced, I then went back after my family and brought them home, and Brother Joseph asked me if we all got back safe and well. I told him that we had gotten home safe, but it was by the blessings of God. He said that he was glad that we had gotten home safe, and he said, "Now go and try it without your family and you shall not be hurt," so I left my family in Nauvoo; they were all pretty well at that time, although they had seen much hardship. They had to live on crabapples and honey for nine weeks and nothing else to eat only what game we could kill once in a while. Well, I started back again with Brother Emmett to the Sioux nation but we had but little success for they did or could not understand the principles of the gospel, so we had to return home again on the fourteenth of February and my wife bore me a daughter and we named her Sarah Adaline.

Autobiography of John Lowe Butler, Typescript, HBLL; http://www.boap.org/

8. d. Orson Pratt

"Orson Pratt served nineteen full-time missions."
The Church News, *June 13, 1948.*

9. True

Two others who enjoyed success were Zebedee Coltrin and Levi Hancock. After leaving Kirtland, they headed south and west along the National road toward Indianapolis, Indiana. Baptisms came slowly at first, but when they reached Winchester, Indiana, they found ready listeners. Levi wrote, "We continued to preach here and in the regions round about until we had raised a large branch of the Church." They enjoyed similar results in Ward township, and "in a short time we had in both places about one hundred members." Their presence aroused a group of local men who accosted them and ordered them to leave the area by ten o'clock the next morning.

The elders decided to stay and keep an eleven o'clock appointment. Some of the men who appeared for the meeting were among the ones who had threatened the missionaries. In his sermon Levi said that his father had fought in the Revolutionary War for the freedom his listeners then enjoyed and that his relative, John Hancock, was

the first signer of the Declaration of Independence. Levi recorded,
"After the meeting we went to the water and baptized seventeen out
of those who the day before were going to mob us."

*"The Life of Levi Hancock," unpublished manuscript, Brigham Young
University, Special Collections, Provo, Utah, 54–64.*

MORMON TRAIL

1. Jonathan Crosby relates in his autobiography how his wagon was so stuck in the mud that nothing could get it out. To his amazement, though, something came down the trail that helped to dislodge his wagon. What was it?
   a. Curious Natives that wanted to lend a helping hand
   b. The Missouri mob, wanting to help
   c. An unattended yoke of oxen
   d. John Deere

2. What was it pioneer John Alger wanted to trade to a young Sioux Chief for a horse?
   a. A sixteen-year-old pioneer girl
   b. Beads
   c. Flour
   d. Two cows

3. What did Patience Archer see while pulling her handcart?
   a. Angels pushing the handcart in front of her
   b. A group of Natives wanting to assist the tired, worn out pioneers
   c. A strange man giving news that the rescue party was just over the next hill
   d. The Salt Lake Temple constantly in her view

4. True or false? It took longer to cross the 310 miles across the State of Iowa than it did to travel the 1100 miles from Winter Quarters to the Salt Lake Valley.

5. How did one woman describe the four young men that carried the Willie Handcart Company across the Sweet Water River?
   a. "Very strong, courageous souls"
   b. "Rather rough in their manners, but kind good hearts"
   c. "Four angels sent by God"
   d. "A fine catch for any young lady"

6. Mary Powell Sabin states that when the handcart company she was traveling in entered Salt Lake City, they were offered what to eat?
   a. Corn dogger (corn bread)
   b. Apples and bread
   c. Molasses and bread
   d. Watermelon

7. Sarah James, member of the Willie Handcart Company, told her mother she was going to cook what?
   a. Cow hide
   b. Her shoes
   c. Beef stew
   d. The leather straps used to tie down their load on the handcart

8. How did the Saints cross the deeper rivers on the trail?
   a. Everyone held hands
   b. They floated across in the company boat
   c. They built rafts
   d. They rode on the backs of the cattle

9. What did Mosiah Hancock kill on the prairies while in search of the family cow and calf?
   a. A rattlesnake
   b. A grizzly bear
   c. A panther
   d. A buffalo

ANSWERS

1. c. An unattended yoke of oxen

During our first day's travel we came to a bad slue crossing in the road, and we got stuck fast so that we were compelled to unload in order to get out, but even then our team was not able to pull the empty wagon out. But just then, a large, fine yoke of oxen came along the road behind us overtaking us, unattended by any person, and which we considered very providential aid. So I hitched them on the wagon with my own team, and pulled out easily. I then turned the strange oxen loose again, loaded in the things we had taken out, and traveled on. We looked upon that aid and help as being directly from our Heavenly Father. After that, we got stuck in bad places several times, and had to unload in order to pull out but only a few days passed, and Brother Ezra Clark with a small company overtook us, and then we had no more trouble. When we came to bad places, we were in duty bound to help each other.

Autobiography of Jonathan Crosby, Typescript, Utah State Historical Society. Holograph is also located in the Utah State Historical Society; http://www.boap.org/

2. a. A sixteen-year-old pioneer girl

"When we got to within about two day's travel of Laramie, we just about got into some trouble with a large company of Sioux Indians. John Alger started in fun to trade a sixteen-year-old girl to a young Chief for a horse. But the Chief was in earnest! We got the thing settled, however, and were permitted to go without the loss of Lovina."

Autobiography of Mosiah Hancock, Typescript, BYU-S; http://www.boap.org/

3. c. A strange man giving news that the rescue party was just over the next hill

The following from the journal of Patience Loader Rozsa Archer who was a member of the ill-fated Martin Handcart Company:

I will say we traveled on all day in the snow but the weather was fine and in the middle of the day the sun was quite warm. Sometime in the afternoon a strange man appeared to me as we was resting as we got up the hill. He came and looked in my face. He said is you Patience. I said yes. He said again I thought it was you. Travel on.

There is help for you. You will come to a good place. There is plenty. With this he was gone. He disappeared. I looked but never saw where he went. This seemed very strange to me. I took this as someone sent to encourage us and give us strength.

Kenneth W. Godfrey, Audrey M. Godfrey, and Jill Mulvay Derr, Women's Voices: An Untold History of the Latter-day Saints 1830–1900 *(Salt Lake City: Deseret Book, 1982), 231.*

Actually Natives did help pull the handcarts on at least a few occasions. John Parry wrote in his journal, "Indians met us some times and helped us to pull our Carts, which was a great fun for them."

David Roberts, Devils Gate—Brigham Young and the Great Mormon Handcart Tragedy *(New York City: Simon and Schuster, 2008), 124.*

4. True

It took the Saints 131 days to cross the 310 miles of Iowa to Winter Quarters but only 111 days to trek the 1000 miles from Winter Quarters to the Salt Lake Valley.

Our Heritage *(Salt Lake City: The Church of Jesus Christ of Latter-day Saints, 1996), 71.*

5. b. "Rather rough in their manners, but kind good hearts"

We have all heard the story of the four young men who carried the members of the Martin Handcart Company across the ice-filled Sweet Water River. Patience Loader sheds some more light on this story. The following from her journal:

> We traveled on for some few miles. Then we came to the Sweet Water. There we had to cross. We thought we would have to wade the water as the cattle had been crossing with the wagons with the tents and what little flour we had and had broken the ice so we could not go over on the ice. But there was three brave men [actually there were four] there in the water packing the women and children over on their backs. Names William Kimball, Ephraim Hanks, and I think the other was James Furgeson. [Either this is another incident or else she recorded the names wrong. The four young men were George W. Grant, C. A. Huntington, David P. Kimball, and Stephen W. Taylor.] Those poor brethren was in the water nearly all day. We wanted to thank them but they would not listen to us. My dear Mother felt in her heart to bless them for their kindness. She said

God bless you for taking me over this water and in such an awful rough way. They said oh d— that I don't want any of that. You are welcome. We have come to help you. Mother turned to me saying what do [you] think of that man. He is a rough fellow. I told her that is Brother William Kimball. I am told they are all good men but I daresay that they are all rather rough in their manners. But we found that they all had kind good hearts. This poor Brother Kimball stayed so long in the water that he had to be taken out and packed to camp and he was a long time before he recovered as he was chilled through and in after life he was always afflicted with rheumatism.

Kenneth W. Godfrey, Audrey M. Godfrey, and Jill Mulvay Derr, Women's Voices: An Untold History of The Latter-day Saints 1830–1900 *(Salt Lake City: Deseret Book, 1982), 236.*

6. d. Watermelon

Mary Powell Sabin, a twelve-year-old Welsh girl traveling in the Ellsworth handcart company, stated that at the celebration of their company's arrival into Salt Lake City the first food they were offered was watermelons. Brigham Young instructed the emigrants to just eat the pink and not to go into the green of the melon.

David Roberts, Devils Gate—Brigham Young and the Great Mormon Handcart Tragedy *(New York City: Simon and Schuster, 2008), 113.*

7. b. Her shoes

The following from Sarah James, a member of the Willie Handcart Company:

> Father told us one night that the flour was gone. . . . Father was white and drawn. I knew that mother was worried about him, for he was getting weaker all the time and seemed to feel that there was no use in all the struggle. Captain Willie announced one morning that all the animals in the company would be killed for fresh meat. We were so hungry that we didn't stop to think what it would do for our wagons. How good the soup tasted made from the bones of those cows, although there wasn't any fat on them. The hides we used to roast after taking all the hair off of them. I even decided to cook the tatters of my shoes and make soup of them. I brought a smile to my father's sad face when I made the suggestion, but mother was a bit impatient with me and told me that I'd have to eat the muddy things myself.

Heidi Swinton and Lee Groberg, Sweetwater Rescue: The Willie and Martin Handcart Story *(American Fork, Utah: Covenant, 2006), 71.*

The following story gives us further indication of the hunger suffered by the young during the fall of 1856:

> John Bond, a twelve-year-old in the Hodgett Wagon Train with his family, later recorded, "Day after day passes and still no tidings of help coming from westward. The bugle is sounded again . . . to call all the Saints together for prayers to ask the infinite Father to bring food, medicines, and other things necessary for the sick and needy." Bond had seen a woman cooking a pot of dumplings before evening prayer and then watched her hide them. He did not go to prayer. "I stood back and looked for the dumplings, found them, and being so hungry I could not resist the temptation, sat down and ate them all."

Heidi Swinton and Lee Groberg, Sweetwater Rescue: The Willie and Martin Handcart Story *(American Fork, Utah: Covenant, 2006), 78.*

8. a. Everyone held hands

"As they came to rivers, the captain would go through on horseback, then they would all hold hands and pass through to the other side. No one could ride except the sick and the small children."

Della Henderson Holladay, "Pioneers of Faith, Courage, and Endurance." Chronicles of Courage: Daughters of Utah Pioneers *(Salt Lake City: Utah Printing Company, 1991), 2:75.*

9. c. A panther

> My brother Levi was born the 28th of February—8½ months after my father left for the Battalion. We had a cow that freshened this spring, but she was up to the bottoms, 40 miles away. We tried to get some of the brethren to bring her down, and they said they would. But mother dreamed that Bill Hickman got the cow and calf, and she wished me to see if I could get a horse and saddle. I dreamed, however, that thieves got away with the horse and saddle, so I took my gun, and mother made me three skillets of corn dodger, and the next morning I started out on foot. Mother also gave me three matches so that I could have a fire when I camped. Our bedding being scarce, I did not take a quilt, even though the season wasn't very warm. The first day was so muddy that I got only about 20 miles; but I came to a grove of trees—mostly slippery elm and basswood. I soon had a good fire for the wood was plentiful. I had

my knife along, and I got some elmbark which seemed to go well with my corn bread. I made me a bed with some dry leaves at the foot of a clump of trees, and was soon in a sound sleep. But, a dismal noise awakened me! I grabbed my gun and corn dodger, and up a tree I went, for wolves were in force! I threw some wood on the fire so that the blaze would keep back those "clamoring varmits," as David Crockett would say. Oh, how the cold wind did pierce me! By daylight the wolves were gone, and I left my perch. I soon got warm by the good fire, and I tried to do some praying—for the music in the wolves choir seemed to introduce in me a desire to feel a little religious. I went on and inquired for our cow, but no one seemed to know anything about her. I soon got my eye on her, and started back that evening. I got to a nice wood where I built a fire, and tied the cow with a rope I had found. The calf had been considerable trouble, so I tied it to the cow! Oh, but the wolves were so thick! I had the calf tied to the cow and the cow tied to a tree—then I made a fire close to the cow, then scraped some leaves together for my bed. I got a great pile of wood so I could keep fire through the night. Then I saw a rabbit run up the hollow tree where I intended to lay my head; I reached it with my arm and soon had it skinned and cooked. I had a supper fit for a king with the rabbit, some of the dodger I had left, and some milk I milked into my mouth! The third day of my trip, I arose early and ate the rest of my rabbit and dodger. I found the cow had eaten the pile of straw I carried on my head, which was supposed to be my hat, so I went forth bare headed. However, the day was cloudy, so I didn't suffer with heat. Although the snow was nearly gone, except in the gulches, there was much mud; but I made it to the Perkins settlement, where I and my "companions" fell into good hands. The goodly company seemed to suppose me to be somewhat of a hero. I had a good supper and slept soundly, never once thinking of the wolf choir. The next morning I ate a hearty breakfast, and my kind friends sent me forth with a good lunch. At noon I shot a large grey wolf that got too close, and while going down the Mosquite, a panther put up a sneak job on me and my company—however, I saw its movements as it crouched near the path. I put a ball between its eyes and it quivered without making much of a spring. I then began to cast about for another place to sleep, supposing it would be late before I got the thing skinned; when all at once, Jack Reddin rode up on horseback. He saw the situation and gave me $2.50 for the panther, so I traveled on towards home, reaching it about 12 o'clock midnight, much to the joy of my mother who was waiting and worrying for me. I can assure all, I rested sweetly that night!

Autobiography of Mosiah Hancock, Typescript, BYU-S; http://www. boap.org/

PEOPLE AND PERSONAGES

1. Who did the Lord say was most similar in characteristics to John the Baptist in this dispensation?
   a. Joseph Smith Jr.
   b. Joseph Smith Sr.
   c. Lorenzo Snow
   d. Sidney Rigdon

2. When Joseph Smith asked Sidney Rigdon, Oliver Cowdery, and Zebedee Coltrin to lie in the grass on their backs and view the sky while at a conference in New Portage, Ohio, who appeared to them?
   a. Laman and Lemuel
   b. Adam and Eve
   c. Elijah and Elias
   d. George Washington and Benjamin Franklin

3. We know that the angel Moroni appeared to Joseph Smith and the Three Witnesses and also Mary Whitmer. What other three men were privileged with a visitation from this heavenly personage?
   a. Heber C. Kimball, Oliver Granger, and W. W. Phelps
   b. Heber C. Kimball, John Whitmer, and Parley P. Pratt
   c. Parley P. Pratt, Newell K. Whitney, and W. W. Phelps
   d. Willard Richards, John Taylor, and Hyrum Smith

4. Ziba Peterson was one of four missionaries that were sent to the Lamanites on the western boundaries of Missouri in the early winter of 1830. In 1848 he and his family moved west. What town did he move to?
   a. Florence, Nebraska
   b. Salt Lake City, Utah
   c. Mt. Pishga, Iowa
   d. Hangtown, California

5. Who did Orson Hyde say guided Christopher Columbus in dreams and was present in the camp of George Washington helping to direct the affairs of the Revolutionary War?
   a. The Three Nephites
   b. John the Beloved
   c. The premortal spirits of Joseph Smith and Lorenzo Snow
   d. The angel Moroni

6. The Danites were a band of avengers that plundered and stole from the Missouri mob. What was the original name of the Danites?
   a. Beehives
   b. Stripling Warriors
   c. Daughter of Zion
   d. Army of Helaman

7. According to Wilford Woodruff, which prophet of the Church was at Haun's Mill at the time of the massacre?
   a. Brigham Young
   b. Joseph Smith
   c. John Taylor
   d. Wilford Woodruff

8. What did the Prophet Joseph Smith desire of Brother Coray?
   a. That he would attend his meetings more regularly
   b. That he would give a more generous fast offering
   c. That the two of them could wrestle
   d. That he would break Porter Rockwell out of jail

9. True or false? Only men died in the Haun's Mill Massacre.

10. According to John Lowe Butler, why did one member of the mob stay the night in an LDS home during the siege of Far West?
    a. The militia camp cook made horrible food
    b. It was too cold to stay out of doors
    c. He did not have an issue with the Mormons and wanted to stay at an LDS friend's house
    d. He forgot his rifle cleaning equipment at home and knew he could buy a kit in Far West

11. What did the Missouri militia mob that surrounded Far West do every evening before retiring for the night?
    a. Held evening worship services and said a prayer
    b. Told Mormon jokes and stories around the campfire
    c. Held target practice
    d. Sang as loud as they could, hoping to keep the residents of Far West awake

12. As part of Joseph Smith's tutorial with the angel Moroni on September 22, 1826, he was told that he could take possession of the plates the next year if he brought what with him?
    a. The right person
    b. A container to carry the plates
    c. Lunch because the next visit would last most of the day
    d. A humble and contrite spirit

13. Governor Ford's greatest fear was about how people would think of him in future generations after his failed promise of protection to the Prophet Joseph Smith in Carthage Jail. Who did Governor Ford say people might link him to?
    a. King Noah or Cain
    b. Ramses, Pharaoh of Egypt at the time of Moses
    c. Herod or Pilate
    d. King Henry VIII

14. Porter Rockwell and Joseph Smith were blamed for the attempted murder of ex–Missouri governor Boggs. Which one of the four men listed below could very well be the real culprit?
    a. Colonel George M. Hinkle (Mormon Militia leader and traitor)
    b. General David R. Atchison (Missouri Militia man and lawyer)
    c. General Alexander Doniphan (Missouri Militia man and lawyer)

d. Stephen Markham (a Porter Rockwell figure, a little rough around the edges but with a good heart)

15. How many miles of land and sea did Harvey Harris Cluff travel during 25 years of missionary service?
   a. 25,000
   b. 80,000
   c. 92,000
   d. 100,000

16. How many Browning (gun) models were manufactured from the time when Latter-day Saint Jonathan Browning first began making guns during the Nauvoo period of the Church to 1979?
   a. 100,000
   b. 500,000
   c. 15 million
   d. Over 30 million

17. True or false? Warren Foote's description of the Missourians' lifestyle and living conditions was favorable.

18. Aside from being a Mormon, who was Gutzon Borglum?
   a. President Lincoln's Secretary of War
   b. The man who directed the carving of Mt. Rushmore
   c. The first rider on the Pony Express
   d. Porter Rockwell's bodyguard

19. The two children born on the ship Brooklyn, which carried a load of Saints from New York City to San Francisco, were named what?
   a. Atlantic and Pacific
   b. Ocean and Island
   c. Anne and Kate
   d. Misty and Tide

20. The first child to be born in the Salt Lake Valley shortly after the Saints arrived was Young Elizabeth Steele. Who is she named after?
   a. Brigham Young and Eliza R. Snow
   b. Susa Young and Elizabeth Barrett Browning (Famous English Poet)
   c. Brigham Young and Queen Elizabeth

d. Lorenzo Young and Elizabeth Whitney (Wife of Newell K. Whitney)

21. When senior apostle Lorenzo Snow was praying in the Salt Lake Temple over his inadequacies, who appeared to him?
    a. Joseph Smith and Brigham Young
    b. Peter
    c. The Savior
    d. Joseph and Hyrum Smith

22. Who appeared to Parley P. Pratt while he was in prison?
    a. His first wife, Thankful, who had died two years earlier
    b. His parents
    c. His grandfather
    d. One of the Three Nephites

23. Who was the first father and son to serve concurrently in the Quorum of the Twelve?
    a. Brigham Young and Brigham Young Jr.
    b. Joseph Smith Sr. and Joseph Smith Jr.
    c. John Henry Smith and George Albert Smith
    d. Jedediah Grant and Heber J. Grant

24. Who set up a dramatic company in Nauvoo?
    a. Vilate Kimball
    b. Lucy Mack Smith
    c. Joseph Smith
    d. Bathsheba Smith

25. Anson Call met General Wilson (a principle character in the Saints being driven from Jackson County) on a steamboat as Anson was moving to Far West. Anson engaged in conversation with the general. During the conversation General Wilson stated that Joe's (Joseph Smith's) career must be stopped. Anson replied that the only way to stop Joe's career was to do what?
    a. Shoot him
    b. Dethrone God
    c. Take away his priesthood
    d. Get rid of the Book of Mormon

26. Mark Twain referred to the Book of Mormon as what?
    a. Intriguing
    b. Heavenly
    c. Chloroform in print
    d. A great sedative

27. Leo Tolstoy, the great Russian novelist, said what about the Church?
    a. It would become the greatest power the world has ever known
    b. Like Daniel's dream it would fill the whole world
    c. It was as insignificant as a drop in a bucket
    d. It was sure to die a slow death

28. Brigham Young is noted for sending out a rescue party to bring in the handcart companies stranded on the Wyoming plains. Brigham Young was not the only individual to do this. In fact, this same situation happened four years earlier. What were the circumstances and who sent out the rescue party?
    a. John Taylor and the rescuing of the sugar beet equipment
    b. Heber C. Kimball and the rescuing of stranded missionaries on the Mormon Trail
    c. Porter Rockwell and the rescuing of a scouting party sent into the Cache Valley
    d. Willard Richards and the rescuing of a group of Saints taken hostage at Fort Bridger by the US Army

29. Which US President's wife was at the trial of Joseph Smith where he was accused of the assassination attempt of ex-Missouri governor Boggs?
    a. Andrew Jackson's wife
    b. Martin Van Buren's wife
    c. James K. Polk's wife
    d. Abraham Lincoln's wife

30. What caused apostate John Sermon to come back to the Church?
    a. Hearing Martin Harris's testimony
    b. Visiting the Nauvoo temple site after the temple burned
    c. Spending a week with Porter Rockwell
    d. Visiting the Sacred Grove

31. Who wrote about the escapades of apostate George Adams?
    a. W. W. Phelps

b. Solomon Spaulding
c. John Wentworth
d. Mark Twain

ANSWERS

1. d. Sidney Rigdon

The Lord compared Sidney Rigdon to John the Baptist. This was previous to Sidney Rigdon separating himself from the Church.

Church History in the Fulness of Times *(Salt Lake City: The Church of Jesus Christ of Latter-day Saints), 82.*

2. b. Adam and Eve

Once after returning from a mission, he [Zebedee Coltrin] met Brother Joseph in Kirtland, who asked him if he did not wish to go with him to a conference at New Portage. The party consisted of Presidents Joseph Smith, Sidney Rigdon, Oliver Cowdery and myself [Zebedee Coltrin]. Next morning at New Portage, he noticed that Joseph seemed to have a far off look in his eyes, or was looking at a distance and presently he, Joseph, stepped between Brothers Cowdery and Coltrin and taking them by the arm, said, "Let's take a walk." They went to a place where there was some beautiful grass and grapevines and swampbeech interlaced. President Joseph Smith then said, "Let us pray." They all three prayed in turn—Joseph, Oliver, and Zebedee. Brother Joseph then said, "Now brethren, we will see some visions." Joseph lay down on the ground on his back and stretched out his arms and the two brethren lay on them. The heavens gradually opened, and they saw a golden throne, on a circular foundation, something like a light house, and on the throne were two aged personages, having white hair, and clothed in white garments. They were the two most beautiful and perfect specimens of mankind he ever saw. Joseph said, "They are our first parents, Adam and Eve." Adam was a large, broad-shouldered man, and Eve as a woman, was as large in proportion.

Minutes, Salt Lake City School of the Prophets, October 11, 1883.

3. a. Heber C. Kimball, Oliver Granger, and W. W. Phelps

Donl. H. Petersen, Moroni: Ancient Prophet, Modern Messenger
(Bountiful, Utah: Horizon Publishers, 1983), 114–16, 151–52.

4. d. Hangtown, California

Ziba Peterson was one of four missionaries (Oliver Cowdery, Peter
Whitmer Jr., and Parley P. Pratt were the other three) sent on a mission to the Delaware Indians in 1830–31. When the Saints were driven
out of Jackson County in 1833, Ziba stayed, separating himself from
the Church. In 1848 he and his family moved to California, where he
became the sheriff of Dry Diggins, later known as Hangtown because
of the hanging of two thieves that Peterson supervised. He died at
"Hangtown" (known today as Placerville, California) in 1849.

*Dean H. Garrett, "Ziba Peterson: From Missionary to Hanging Sher-
iff."* Nauvoo Journal *19 (Spring 1997), 24–32.*

5. d. The angel Moroni

Elder Orson Hyde taught something interesting pertaining
to Moroni. He referred to Moroni as the "Prince of America" and
said that he "presides over the destinies of America, and feels a lively
interest in all our doings." Elder Hyde went on to say that Moroni
helped guide Christopher Columbus through dreams and visions,
was in the camp of George Washington directing affairs by an invis-
ible hand, and led our founding fathers on to victory, "and all this to
open and prepare the way for the Church and kingdom of God to be
established on the western hemisphere, for the redemption of Israel
and the salvation of the world."

Journal of Discourses, *26 vols. (London: Latter-day Saints' Book
Depot, 1854–86), 6:368.*

6. c. Daughter of Zion

A Dr. Sampson Avard organized the Danites. This group of avengers' purpose was to plunder and murder the enemies of the Church in
Missouri. The original name of this group of outlaws was "The Daughter of Zion." When the Prophet Joseph Smith discovered this, he cut
Dr. Avard off from the Church.

William Edwin Berrett, The Restored Church *(Salt Lake City:
Deseret Book, 1973), 146.*

7. **a. Brigham Young**

The following is related by Wilford Woodruff:

On May 6th, I met with the Seventies, and we ordained sixty men into the quorums of Elders and Seventies. Brother Joseph met with the Twelve, Bishops and Elders, at Bishop Partridge's house; and there were a number with us who were wounded at Haun's Mill. Among them was Isaac Laney, who had been in company with about twenty others, at the mill, when a large armed mob fired among them with rifles and other weapons, and shot down seventeen of the brethren, and wounded more. Brother Laney fled from the scene, but they poured a shower of lead after him, which pierced his body through and through. He showed me eleven bullet holes in his body. There were twenty-seven in his shirt, seven in his pantaloons, and his coat was literally cut to pieces. One ball entered one arm-pit and came out at the other.

Another entered his back and came out at the breast. A ball passed through each hip, each leg and each arm. All these shots were received while he was running for life, and, strange as it may appear, though he had also one of his ribs broken, he was able to outrun his enemies, and his life was saved. We can only acknowledge this deliverance to be by the power and mercy of God.

President Brigham Young was also among the number. He also fled, and although the balls flew around him like hail he was not wounded. How mysterious are the ways of the Lord!

Leaves of My Journal, *Preston Nibley, comp., (Salt Lake City: Book-craft, 1988), 74.*

8. **c. That the two of them could wrestle**

In the following June, I met with an accident, which I shall here mention: The Prophet and myself, after looking at his horses, and admiring them, that were just across the road from his house, we started thither, the Prophet at this same time put his arm over my shoulder. When we had reached about the middle of the road, he stopped and remarked, "Brother Coray, I wish you were a little larger, I would like to have some fun with you." I replied, "Perhaps you can as it is," not realizing what I was saying, Joseph a man of over 200 pounds weight, while I scarcely 130 pounds, made it not a little ridiculous for me to think of engaging with him in anything like a scuffle. However, as soon as I made this reply, he began to trip me; he took some kind of a lock on my right leg, from which I was unable to extricate it, and throwing me around, broke it some three inches above the ankle joint. He immediately carried me into the house, pulled off my boot, and found at once that my leg was decidedly broken; then he got some splinters and bandaged it. A number of times that day did he come in to see me, endeavoring to console me as much as possible. The next day when he happened in to see me after a little conversation, I said, "Brother Joseph, when Jacob wrestled with the angel and was lamed by him, the angel blessed him; now I think I am also entitled to a blessing." To that he replied, "I am not the patriarch, but my father is, and when you get up and around, I'll have him bless you." He said no more for a minute or so, meanwhile looking very earnestly at me, then said, "Brother Coray, you will soon find a companion, one that will be suited to your condition and whom you will be satisfied with. She will cling to you, like to cords of death, and you will have a good many children." He also said some other things, which I can't so distinctly remember.

In nine days after my leg was broken, I was able to get up and hobble about the house by the aid of a crutch and in two weeks thereafter, I was about recovered, nearly as well as ever, so much so that I went to meeting on foot, a distance of a mile. I considered this no less than a case of miraculous healing. For nothing short of three months did I think it would be ere I should be around again, on my feet, able to resume work.

Autobiography of Martha Jane Coray, Typescript, HBLL; LDS Church Archives; http://www.boap.org/

9. False

It has been said that only men were killed at Haun's Mill. According to John P. Greene, at least one female also died. "Miss Mary Stedwell while fleeing was shot through the hand, and, fainting, fell over a log, into which they shot upwards of twenty balls."

John P. Greene, Facts Relative to the Expulsion of the Mormons or Latter-day Saints, From the State of Missouri, Under the Exterminating Order *(Cincinnati: R. P. Brooks, 1839).*

10. c. He did not have an issue with the Mormons and wanted to stay at an LDS friend's house

The following is a story from the journal of John Lowe Butler:

When the mob came to Far West there [was a man] by the name of Nathan and [I was] well acquainted with him. He would not volunteer to come and fight the Mormons so they drafted him and made him come and just before they got to Far West the captain told the men to cut a whole lot of switches to hang them on their saddle so that if the Mormons should whip them out they would have something to make the horses faster, but Nathan did not get any switches and they said, "Why do you not get some, Nathan?" His answer was, "I have no cause for any for I have never done the Mormons any harm and they will not do me any harm." So when they got to camp and the baggage wagon had come up, Nathan said that he was going over to the city to see an old friend of his and they told him that the Mormons would kill him if he did. He told them that he was not afraid, so he started over to my house, and when he got there he told my mother that he had come to have some supper and stay all night. She asked him who all the men were that had come down on the city. He told her that they were a mob come to kill all the Mormons. "Well," said the old lady, "You have come with them, have you not?" Nathan said he had, but not to kill the Mormons; they had forced him to come to fight them, but they could not force him to shoot and he was going home in the morning.

Well, about three or four hours later there came five or six men to fetch him away. They said that the captain had sent them after him. Nathan told them that he should not go for he could sleep in a house. So he said that they could go and tell their captain so. Well, they went back and Nathan slept. He had his breakfast in the morning and told the folks that if the mob drove the Mormons away, his house would be a home for them as long as they had a mind to stay. Well, he wished them good luck and started, but not back to the camp, but back home. Now the captain sent over in the day to see where he was, they inquired of my mother where he was and she told them that he had gone home, so they had to go back without him.

Autobiography of John Lowe Butler, Typescript, HBLL; http://www. boap.org/

11. a. Held evening worship services and said a prayer
The following from the journal of William Draper:

I will here relate a short conversation that took place between a little boy about twelve years old by the name of Buduas Dustin and a Methodist preacher; and captain of a company and chaplain for the army by the name of [Samuel] Bogard, which took place as follows:

One evening when the little boy was present the army was called to order to attend evening services and a solemn prayer and thanks to their unknown God for the glorious works that he was permitting and assisting them to perform, and when the prayer was finished the boy stood as if in deep meditation and said, "Mr. Bogard can I ask you one question?" "Yes boy," was the answer, and the boy proceeded by saying, "Mr. Bogard, sir, which way do you think is right for a person to have their eyes closed or open when they pray?" "Well my boy I suppose either would be acceptable if done in humility but it looks more humiliating to have our eyes closed against the transitory objects around us and from the world." "Well," said the boy, "I think if I was engaged in such a work as you are I should want my eyes open." "Why, my boy," was the inquiry. "Because I should fear the devil would carry me off if they were shut."

They then threatened his life for a young Mormon; but he said, "I am no Mormon," and he was not and so he escaped but subsequently joined the church.

Autobiography of William Draper, Typescript, HBLL; http://www. boap.org/

12. a. The right person

I find it of interest that on all occasions when Joseph visited the angel Moroni at the Hill Cumorah he ventured alone, with the exception of September 22, 1827. That day Joseph brought Emma, his young wife with him. The answer of why he did this can be found in the previous year's tutorial between Moroni and Joseph. Moroni told Joseph on this occasion that the plates would be given to him if he "brought the right person." Moroni also told Joseph that he would know who that person would be.

Obviously Joseph listened to the Spirit and brought the "right" person with him on his next and last visit to the Hill Cumorah.

Alexander L. Baught, "Parting the Veil: The Visions of Joseph Smith." BYU Studies, *Vol. 38, No. 1, p. 31.*

13. c. Herod or Pilate

Thomas Ford, governor of the state of Illinois at the time of the martyrdom, had this to say:

> The murder of the Smiths, instead of putting an end to . . . the Mormons and dispersing them, as many believed it would, only bound them together closer than ever, gave them new confidence in their faith. . . . Some gifted man like Paul, some splendid orator who will be able by his eloquence to attract crowds of the thousands . . .

may succeed in breathing a new life into [the Mormon Church] and make the name of the martyred Joseph ring ... loud and stir the souls of men.

It was Governor Ford's greatest fear that his name would become a Pilate or Herod, forever mentioned in history as a villain of the innocent, "dragged down to posterity." Needless to say, this was all fulfilled due to his own merits.

Thomas Ford, A History of Illinois, *Milo Milton Quaife, ed., 2 vols. (1946), 2:217, 221–23.*

14. b. General David R. Atchison (Missouri Militia man and lawyer)

When the trouble with the mob commenced, Colonel Robinson took about one-half of the force to Adam-ondi-Ahman to defend that place. Joseph, Hyrum and Sidney also went with them, leaving me in command at Far West. The detachment returned in about four days.

A few days afterwards Joseph Smith and I took a walk out upon the prairie, and in the course of our conversation I suggested to him to send for General [David R.] Atchison to defend him in the suit then brought against him, as he was in command of the third division of the militia of the State of Missouri, and was a lawyer and a friend to law. Joseph made no reply, but turned back immediately to Far West, and a man was selected, with the best horse to be found, to go to Liberty for General Atchison.

The next day General Atchison came to Far West with a hundred men and camped a little north of the town.

On consulting with Joseph Smith, Atchison told him that he did not want anyone to go with them to his trial, which was to take place midway between Far West and Adam-ondi-Ahman. Joseph at first hesitated about agreeing to this, but Atchison reassured him by saying: "My life for yours!"

When they arrived at the place of trial quite a number of the mob had gathered, and on seeing Joseph commenced to curse and swear. Atchison, however, checked them by saying: "Hold on boys, if you fire the first gun there will not be one of you left!"

Joseph was cleared and came away unmolested. Soon afterwards the governor, thinking Atchison was too friendly towards the Saints, took his command from him and placed General [John B.] Clark in command of the militia.

Shortly before Far West was besieged, I was taken sick, and Colonel [George M.] Hinkle came into military command under his old commission. I gave up my horse, saddle and bridle, and also my rifle and sword for Brother Lysander Gee to use in defense of our city. When General Clark's army came up against Far West, Colonel Hinkle betrayed the First Presidency of the Church into their hands for seven hundred and fifty dollars. Then Joseph and Hyrum [Smith], Sidney [Rigdon], and Lyman Wight were taken by the mob, who held a court-martial over them and sentenced them to be shot the next morning at eight o'clock on the public square. Lyman Wight told them to "shoot and be damned." Generals Atchison and [Alexander W.] Doniphan immediately rebelled against the decision, and Doniphan said, if men were to be murdered in cold blood, he would withdraw his troops, which he did. General Atchison then went to Liberty and gave a public dinner, and delivered a speech, in which he said, "If the governor does not restore my commission to me, I will kill him, so help me God!" On hearing this the audience became so enthusiastic that they took him upon their shoulders and carried him around the public square.

Early Scenes in Church History, Four Faith Promoting Classics *(Salt Lake City: Bookcraft, 1968), 74–96.*

15. d. 100,000

The following is from the autobiography of Harvey Harris Cluff: "Twenty-five years of missionary labors and travelling over one hundred thousand miles by land and sea."

Autobiography of Harvey Harris Cluff; http://www.boap.org/

16. d. Over 30 million

During the Nauvoo period of the Church, Jonathan Browning (famous gun manufacturer) became a member and set up shop. In 1852 he moved west with the Saints and settled in Ogden. In 1855 his first child was born after their arrival in the Ogden area. This child would become world-famous gunmaker John Moses Browning. The following from *John M. Browning, American Gunmaker*:

His accomplishments are remarkable, whether they are measured by their innovations, their number, their duration, or their popularity. During those forty-seven inventive years, John M. Browning was issued 128 different patents, to cover a total of some eighty complete and distinct firearm models. They include practically every caliber from the .22-short cartridge through the 37-mm. projectile; they embrace automatic actions, semi-automatic actions, lever actions, and pump actions; they include guns that operate by gas pressure, by both the short and long recoil principle, and by the blowback principle; they include models utilizing sliding locks, rotating locks and vertical locks. Included among them are most of the successful sporting arms which appeared during this period, as well as many of the military arms. It is estimated that well over thirty million Browning designed guns have been produce to date (1979), by Browning, Winchester, Colt, Fabrique Nationale, Remington, Savage, and others.

Paul A. Curtis, John M. Browning, American Gunmaker *(Garden City, New York: Doubleday and Company, 1964), 219.*

17. **False**

The following is Warren Foote's description of the inhabitants of Missouri:

> The inhabitants of Missouri came from the southern states. The most of them are very ignorant, being unable to read, and write. Although the soil is so exceedingly rich, they raise but little grain; a patch of corn, and a drove of hogs running wild in the woods, is the height of their ambition. The corn makes their corndodger, and the hogs their bacon. Corndodger, bacon, and buttermilk, or clabber, constitutes the chief food of the lower classes, and in fact the upper classes do not live much better. Sometimes they have a little wheat flour, but they do not know how to make bread of it, being unacquainted with yeast, or saleratus. They appear to be the offscourings of the southern states. Their clothes are ragged dirty and filthy, and one would hardly know them from the savages of the forest, by their appearance. There are some of a better class who dress well and appear neat and clean. They are all very kind, and hospitable to strangers, and will set before them the best they have. They salt their pork in a corner of their house until it gets salt enough to make bacon, they then hang it in a smoke house, and smoke it a very little, but during the summer it often gets full of life, but they do not mind that. Wild bees being very plentiful, they generally have more or less honey. They have a dislike to eastern, and northern people, they call them all Yankees.

Autobiography of Warren Foote, Typescript, HBLL; http://www.boap. org/

18. b. The man who directed the carving of Mt. Rushmore

"Gutzon Borglum, the man who directed the carving of Mt. Rushmore, is the son of Danish immigrants who entered Salt Lake City in 1864."

Paul B. Skousen, The Skousen Book of Mormon World Records *(Springville, Utah: Cedar Fort, 2004), 195.*

19. a. Atlantic and Pacific

"The ship Brooklyn, which sailed from New York City to California in 1847, carried 70 men, 68 women, and 100 children. During the 17,000 mile journey, there were 12 deaths and two births. The names of the two children born were Atlantic and Pacific."

Our Heritage, The Church of Jesus Christ of Latter-day Saints *(Salt Lake City: The Church of Jesus Christ of Latter-day Saints, 1996), 74.*

20. c. Brigham Young and Queen Elizabeth

"The first child born to the Saints shortly after they entered the valley was a girl born to John and Catherine Steele. They named her Young Elizabeth after Brigham Young and Queen Elizabeth."

Edward W. Tullidge, The Women of Mormondom *(New York: Tullidge and Crandall, 1877), 443.*

21. c. The Savior

Now that Wilford Woodruff had passed away the burden of leading the Church fell on the shoulders of the senior Apostle in the Quorum of the Twelve, Lorenzo Snow. One day while praying in the temple, pouring out his heart about his concerns and what he felt were his inadequacies, he waited for a manifestation, but none came. As he arose and walked through the Celestial room towards his office, the Savior appeared to Lorenzo Snow and told him to reorganize the First Presidency immediately.

Francis M. Gibbons, Dynamic Disciples: Prophets of God *(Salt Lake City: Deseret Book, 1996), 127–28; LeRoi C. Snow, "Remarkable Manifestations to Lorenzo Snow."* Deseret News, *2 April 1938, 8.*

22. a. His first wife, Thankful, who had died two years earlier

The following from the journal of Parley P. Pratt:

After some days of prayer and fasting, and seeking the Lord on the subject, I retired to my bed in my lonely chamber at an early hour, and while the other prisoners and the guard were chatting and beguiling the lonesome hours in the upper apartment of the prison, I lay in silence, seeking and expecting an answer to my prayer, when suddenly I seemed carried away in the spirit. . . . A heaven of peace and calmness pervaded my bosom; a personage from the world of spirits stood before me with a smile of compassion in every look, and pity mingled with the tenderest love and sympathy in every expression of the countenance. A soft hand seemed placed within my own, and a glowing cheek was laid in tenderness and warmth upon mine. A well known voice saluted me, which I readily recognized as that of the wife of my youth, who had for near two years been sweetly sleeping where the wicked cease from troubling and the weary are at rest. I was made to realize that she was sent to commune with me, and answer my question.

Knowing this, I said to her in a most earnest and inquiring tone: "Shall I ever be at liberty again in this life and enjoy the society of my family and the Saints, and Preach the gospel as I have done?" She answered definitely and unhesitatingly: "YES!" I then recollected that I had agreed to be satisfied with the knowledge of that one fact, but now I wanted more.

Said I "Can you tell me how, or by what means, or when I shall escape?" She replied: "That thing is not made known to me yet." I instantly felt that I had gone beyond my agreement and my faith in asking this last question, and that I must be content at present with the answer to the first.

Her gentle spirit then saluted me and withdrew. I came to myself. The doleful noise of the guards, and the wrangling and angry words of the old apostate again grated on my ears, but Heaven and hope were in my soul.

Scot Facer Proctor and Maurine Jensen Proctor, The Autobiography of Parley P. Pratt *(Salt Lake City: Deseret Book, 2000), 295–97.*

23. c. John Henry Smith and George Albert Smith

"In October 1903, George Albert Smith is ordained an Apostle, replacing Brigham Young Jr., who had died. He becomes the first son to serve concurrently with his father (Elder John Henry Smith) in the Quorum of the Twelve Apostles."

Richard Neitzel Holzapfel et al., On This Day in the Church *(Salt Lake City: Eagle Gate, 2000), 196.*

24. c. Joseph Smith

"Joseph Smith set up a dramatic company in Nauvoo, and among those who took part in the plays were Brigham Young, Erastus Snow, and George A. Smith."

Chronicles of Courage, Daughters of Utah Pioneers *(Salt Lake City; Utah Printing Company, 1990) 1:158*

25. b. Dethrone God

While passing up the Missouri River there was a gentleman who came to our room and said that he had learned there were Mormons on the boat. Brother Smith spoke: "Yes, we are Mormons. . . ." The gentleman said, "Where are you going?" "To Far West, sir," was the reply. The man then remarked, "I am sorry to see so respectable a looking company journeying to that place." Brother Smith said, "Why so?" He replied, "Because you will be driven from there before six months." "By whom?" "By the Missourians, gentlemen," said he. My father spoke and said, "Are there not human beings in that country as well as others?" He said, "Gentlemen, I presume you are not aware of the gentleman you are talking to." The reply was, "A Missourian, I presume." The gentleman again spoke, "Yes, gentlemen, I am Colonel Wilson of Jackson County. I was one of the principal actors in driving the Mormons from that county and expect to be soon engaged in driving them from Caldwell County."

He advised us to stop in some other place, for if we went to Far West we were surely to be butchered. We told him we were no better than our brethren and if they died, we were willing to die with them. "Gentlemen," he said, "You appear to be very determined in your minds. Mormonism must and shall be put down." He read to us a letter which he had just received from Newell, which consisted of a bundle of falsehoods concerning our people in Kirtland. "Thrice as false, Joe's career must and shall be stopped." He then started for the door. I then remarked, "If you will stop a moment or two, I will tell you the way it can be done, for there is but one way of accomplishing it." "What is that, sir?" he said. I answered, "Dethrone the Almighty and Joe's career is ended and never until then." He left us very abruptly.

Autobiography of Anson Call, Typescript, HBLL; http://www.boap. org/

26. c. Chloroform in print

Mark Twain had the following to say about the Book of Mormon and Joseph Smith in chapter sixteen of his book *Roughing It*:

All men have heard of the Mormon Bible, but few except the "elect" have seen it, or, at least, taken the trouble to read it. I brought away a copy from Salt Lake. The book is a curiosity to me, it is such a pretentious affair, and yet so "slow," so sleepy; such an insipid mess of inspiration. It is chloroform in print. If Joseph Smith composed this book, the act was a miracle—keeping awake while he did it was, at any rate, if he, according to tradition, merely translated it from certain ancient and mysteriously engraved plates of copper, which he declares he found under a stone, in an out-of-the-way locality, the work of translating was equally a miracle, for the same reason. . . . Whenever he found his speech growing too modern—which was about every sentence of two—he ladled in a few such scriptural phases as "exceeding sore," "and it came to pass," etc., and made things satisfactory again. "And it came to pass" was his pet. If he had left that out, his Bible would have been only a pamphlet."

Mark Twain (Samuel Clemens), Roughing It *(Hartford, Connecticut: American Publishing Company, 1891), 128–29.*

27. a. It would become the greatest power the world has ever known

Leo Tolstoy (1828–1910), the great Russian novelist, had this to say: "If Mormonism is able to endure, unmodified, until it reaches the third and fourth generation, it is destined to become the greatest power the world [has] ever known."

The Church News, *November 16, 1991.*

28. a. John Taylor and the rescuing of the sugar beet equipment

Elder Taylor was instrumental, along with Brigham Young, in introducing the sugar industry to the Utah Territory. On July 4, 1852, a fifty-two wagon train left Fort Leavenworth, Kansas, pulled by two hundred oxen with the sugar beet equipment. This wagon train, as it neared Utah got caught in snows two feet deep. Supplies were running short enough that the men started to consume the oxen. The heavier equipment was being stashed along the trail, to come back [for] at a later date. For now, survival was the imminent priority for these men. When Elder John Taylor, who was a part of the caravan, realized the seriousness of the situation he preceded the wagon train to Salt Lake and sent out a rescue party to bring in the caravan.

William Edwin Berrett, The Restored Church *(Salt Lake City: Deseret Book, 1973), 303.*

29. d. Abraham Lincoln's wife

"One of the ladies to attend the trial of Joseph Smith in connection with the assassination attempt of Lilburn W. Boggs was Mary Todd Lincoln who had just married Abraham Lincoln two months earlier."

Isaac Newton Arnold, "Reminiscences of the Illinois Bar Forty Years Ago" (1881), 5–7; Wasp *(Nauvoo), January 14, 1843, 1.*

30. a. Hearing Martin Harris's testimony

I at one time took a couple of apostates, Henry and John Sermon, to see Martin Harris and to talk to him. One of them asked Mr. Harris if he believed the Book of Mormon to be true, and he told them, "No." They told him they had heard that he had never denied the truth of the Book [of Mormon]. He told them that he knew it was true and that was past believing. After that John Sermon went to Salt Lake City, joined the Church and married a bishops's daughter and lived a good life after.

John Thompson, Autobiography, HBLL, 8–9.

31. d. Mark Twain

George Adams is responsible for the conversion of hundreds of converts but yet is an apostate to the church and was excommunicated. Shortly after the death of the prophet Joseph Smith, he affiliated with James J. Strang, but also was excommunicated. In 1861 he founded the Church of the Messiah in New England and in 1866 moved to the Holy Land; Mark Twain described his encounter with the imperiled colony in his book *Innocents Abroad*. Adams eventually returned to the United States and died at Philadelphia in May 1880.

Peter Amann, "Prophet in Zion: The Saga of George J. Adams." New England Quarterly *37 (1967), 477–500; Reed M. Holmes and G. J. Adams.* The Forerunners *(Independence, MO: Herald House, 1981), 19–53; Arnold K. Garr, Donald Q. Cannon, and Richard O. Cowan,* Encyclopedia of Latter-day Saint History *(Salt Lake City: Deseret Book, 2000), 9.*

PERSECUTIONS

1. How did Joseph Smith and Sidney Rigdon escape while they were being held for a mock trial in a tavern in Painesville, Ohio?
   a. The mob left a window open
   b. The tavern owner was a member
   c. The guard fell asleep
   d. The mob forgot to inform a judge and had to release the prisoners

2. When the mob looked into Far West from a distance, they saw something that frightened them out of attacking the city for a time. What was it?
   a. Ten cannons pointed right at them
   b. The Saints forming an alliance with the local natives
   c. An army totaling thousands of men
   d. The city circled in fire and protected by heavenly angels

3. When the State of Missouri demanded that the Church turn in their weapons, the Hancock brothers refused. Between the three brothers, they had sixteen guns. What else was made to protect them from the mob?
   a. Tomahawks
   b. Bows and arrows
   c. Swords
   d. Pepper spray

4. The Missouri persecutions began in 1833 but would have commenced a year earlier if not for the influence of one non-Mormon. Who was he?
   a. Lilburn W. Boggs (future Missouri Governor)
   b. Alexander Doniphan (friend of the Mormons, Militia General, and lawyer
   c. General Clark (Government Indian Agent)
   d. Judge King (Judge during the trial of Joseph Smith and other Church leaders in Richmond, Missouri)

5. The Battle of Crooked River is noted for two things. What are they?
   a. The opposing military commanders were both officers in the state militia and both were ecclesiastical leaders
   b. The opposing military commanders were brothers and both were raised as pacifists
   c. It was the first time the Missouri militia was called to arms and the first time in the state of Missouri the fight was over religion
   d. It was the first time that Natives battled alongside the Mormon settlers and the first time human shields were used

ANSWERS

1. b. The tavern owner was a member

The following is an excerpt from a letter of Mary Fielding to her sister, Mercy:

> I felt much pleased to see Sisters Walton and Snider who arrived here on Saturday about noon, having left Brother Joseph Smith and Rigdon about 20 miles from Fareport [Fairport, Ohio,] to evade the mobbers. They were to come home in Dr. [Sampson] Avards carriage and expected to arrive about 10 o'clock at night but to their great disappointment they were prevented in a most grievous manner. They had got within 4 miles of home after a very fatiguing journey, much pleased with their visit to Canada and greatly anticipating the pleasure of seeing their homes and families, when they were surrounded with a mob and taken back to Painesville and secured as was supposed in a tavern where they intended to hold a mock trial. But to the disappointment of the wretches the housekeeper was a member of the church who assisted our beloved brethren in making their escape, but as Brother Joseph Smith says not by a basket let down through a window, but by the kitchen door.

Kenneth W. Godfrey and Audrey M. Godfrey, and Jill Mulvay Derr, Women's Voices *(Salt Lake City: Deseret Book Co., 1982), 60–68.*

2. c. An army totaling thousands of men

The following refers to the mob looking into Far West just prior to the Battle of Far West:

> They came on the direction of our city; which produced some little stir in the place, and in a few minutes there was about two hundred men both old and young, mustered to the public square in the city; the rest of the men living absent. We were immediately marched to the south boundary line of the city in the direction of the mob to defend our wives and children and property from destruction. When we arrived to our post the mob was coming down on to a low piece of ground on the boarders of Goose Creek where there was some scattering timber that took them out of our sight but some of them climbed up in to the trees and looked over into the city and swore that they saw an army of men that would number thousands. This we learned from our brethren that was prisoner then in their camp; the sight of this great army brought

terror to their camp which caused them to halt for a little time.
Autobiography of William Draper, Typescript, HBLL; http://www.boap.org/

3.   a. Tomahawks

It is a fact which should be remembered. . . . The Hancock brothers, Levi, Joseph, and Solomon, with their guns, guarded and fed 600 men, women, and children while camped in the woods after they had been driven from their homes. They were waiting for an opportunity to get away. I saw the Prophet marched away; and I saw, oh, the scenes I witnessed! I do not think people would believe them, so I will forbear. The howling fiends, although they wore the uniforms of the U.S., they were not to be trusted! So some of the brethren made three hundred tomahawks for protection.
Autobiography of Mosiah Hancock, Typescript, BYU-S; http://www.boap.org/

4.   c. General Clark (Government Indian Agent)

The persecutions in Jackson County started in 1833. It would have begun a year earlier in 1832, except that a non-Mormon Indian agent put a stop to it. The following from the *Times and Seasons*:

As the church increased the hostile spirit of the people increased also—The enemies circulated from time to time, all manner of false stories against the saints, hoping thereby to stir up the indignation of others. In the spring of 1832 they began to brick-bat or stone the houses of the saints, breaking in windows, &c., not only disturbing, but endangering the lives of the inmates. In the course of that season a county meeting was called at Independence, to adopt measures to drive our people from the country; but the meeting broke up, without coming to any agreement about them; having had too much confusion among themselves, to do more than to have a few knock-downs, after taking a plentiful supply of whiskey. The result of this meeting may be attributed in part, to the influence of certain patriotic individuals; among whom General Clark, a sub-Indian agent, may be considered as principal. He hearing of the meeting, came from his agency, or from home, some thirty or forty miles distant, a day or two before the meeting.

He appeared quite indignant, at the idea of having the constitution and laws set at defiance, and trodden under foot, by the many trampling upon the rights of the few. He went to certain influential mob characters, and offered to decide the case with them in single combat: he said that it would be better for one or two individuals to die, than for hundreds to be put to death.

Times and Seasons, Vol. 1 No. 2. December, 1839.

5. a. The opposing military commanders were both officers in the state militia and both were ecclesiastical leaders

"The Battle of Crooked River on October 24, 1838, is noted for the fact that two commanders of the Missouri state militia faced off against each other and both were also ecclesiastical leaders. David Patten, a member of the Quorum of the Twelve and Samuel Bogart, a Methodist minister."

James B. Allen and Glen M. Leonard, The Story of the Latter-day Saints *(Salt Lake City: Deseret Book, 1992), 136.*

Pioneer Sickness,
Medicine, and Diet

1. Scurvy was a common disease in Winter Quarters, but the Saints discovered a vegetable growing in abundance right where they were living that was effective in treating it. What was the vegetable?
   a. Carrots
   b. Beets
   c. Turnips
   d. Horseradish

2. Why was scurvy referred to as black leg among the pioneers?
   a. The victim's arms would turn black
   b. Both of the victim's legs would turn black from the knee down
   c. Only one entire leg of the victim would turn black
   d. The victim's arms and legs would turn black

3. In his journal, Warren Foote related that both he and his wife were sick. What terminology did he use to describe his senses at the time?
   a. Stupid
   b. Delirious
   c. Senseless
   d. Off in la-la land

4. In a letter to the Mormon Battalion, Brigham Young told the soldiers to leave what alone whenever they get sick?
   a. Candy
   b. Mild foods and herbs

c. Physical exertion

d. The surgeon's medicine

5. In his autobiography, Mosiah Hancock said he and the rest of his household were so sick that he had to literally crawl back and forth sixty yards from their cabin to get what for the family?
   a. Medicine
   b. Horseradish
   c. Herbs
   d. Water

6. Pioneer Robert Gardner Jr. said he had to boil what so that his family had something to eat?
   a. Soup
   b. Potatoes
   c. A cow's hide
   d. Road kill

7. Mosiah Hancock refers to shoats in his autobiography. What is a shoat?
   a. A pig
   b. A goat
   c. A chicken
   d. A lamb

ANSWERS

1. d. Horseradish

"The Saints were affected much by scurvy, also known as black leg to the pioneers. They knew that potatoes provided a suitable cure, but also discovered, rather than sending a wagon into Missouri for a load of potatoes, that horseradish, growing naturally near Winter Quarters, was just as effective."

William Edwin Berrett, The Restored Church *(Salt Lake City: Deseret Book, 1973), 245.*

2. b. Both of the victim's legs would turn black from the knee down

Pioneer Robert Gardner Jr. explains black leg in his autobiography: "Men that could work had to work nearly night and day, for many of the older was taken with a disease called the black leg and was entirely helpless and many died with it. Their legs from their knees down would get as black as a coal."

Autobiography of Robert Gardner Jr., Typescript, HBLL; http://www. boap.org/

3. a. Stupid

The following from Warren Foote's journal of March 17, 1842: "Saturday morning, when the disease seemed to settle on me for a long spell of sickness. It was the inflammation on my lungs. I now became very stupid. . ." Then on January 12, 1845, Warren describes his wife's sickness: "12th. My wife and I have both been sick with a cold the past week. She is smart again."

Autobiography of Warren Foote, Typescript, HBLL; http://www.boap. org/

4. d. The surgeon's medicine

In a letter from Brigham Young to the Mormon Battalion dated August 19, 1846, Brigham Young writes:

... If you are sick, live by faith, and let the surgeon's medicine alone if you want to live, using only such herbs and mild foods as are at your disposal.

This counsel would make sense as it was the surgeon's medicine that killed Alvin Smith.

Daniel Tyler, A Concise History of the March of the Mormon Battalion *(Salt Lake City: Juvenile Instructor Press, 1885), 146.*

5. d. Water

The water stank in Commerce because of the many sloughs. We were so sick at times that we knew not what to do! Sometimes my parents were so ill they could hardly move, and I would take a quart cup and fill it with water from the spring that was about 60 yards from the house. Then, I being weak, would crawl on my arms and knees, and place the cup of water ahead of me and crawl to it each time I reached it, until I reached the house. Then because of father's feverish distress, I would usually give it to him. The water would disappear before anyone could get scarcely a taste, and looking at the heroic face of my mother, and the innocent face of my little sister Amy, I would repeat the pilgrimage until my knees and elbows would be worn near the bone!

Autobiography of Mosiah Hancock, Typescript, BYU-S.

6. c. A cow's hide

The following relates the menu of those that survived the first winter in the Salt Lake Valley:

This looked very discouraging, one thousand miles from any supplies our provisions fell short on account of taking on one of the pioneers whom we found without any provisions. So we fell from half ration to quarter ration. We tried to help out with weeds and what I could with my gun, hawks, crows, snipes, ducks, cranes and wolves, and thistles, roots and rawhide. I had no cow for I had to kill the only one I had the fall before and we had no milk. I took the dry hide that come of my cow. I scalded it and boiled it and eat it. And believe me this was tough. I have known my wife, Jane, to pick wild onion and violets when they first come up on the hillside for hours at a time, and boiled them and thicken them with a rich gravy made of two spoonful of corn meal that would make just what would lay on a small plate. This made a meal or a dinner for my wife and me and three children, but we were blessed in one thing; our children never cried for bread, and that was a thing I often dreaded, lest a time might come when my children might cry for bread and I have none to give them. But all was quite contented and we enjoyed good health.

Autobiography of Robert Gardner Jr., Typescript, HBLL.

7. a. A pig

The following story is in reference to when the Saints first entered Commerce, Illinois, after being pushed out of Missouri:

> One day father was working on a plow, and several good sized shoats came into the yard and began to root up the garden. We had driven them out three times, and father said, "If you come in here once more, I will kill you with a hewing!" I went into a thicket and prayed that father would take a good sized chunk and kill one of those pigs. They did come in again, and father picked up a good sized chunk he had just hewed off a plough beam and threw it with unerring accuracy—hitting mr. piggy right between the eyes, and knocking him dead! Father groaned out, "I am undone!" Then he grabbed the shoat by one leg and started about town to tell of his misfortune. He could not find the owner though, so he anchored the pig at Squire Well's, telling him of his trouble. Whereupon, the worthy Squire said, "Mr. Hancock, you cannot find the owner, so take the pig home and make good use of it." Father brought it home, and it weighed some 80 or 90 pounds! Mother skinned the shoat— then told father not to worry over such small matters. But the rest of the shoats did not seem satisfied, so they came back again! The same boy made another prayer, and the same arm threw the same piece of wood—and another shoat died right there—and mother skinned another shoat! We were all happy as long as the meat lasted. I always felt that God opened the way for us to get something to eat.

Autobiography of Mosiah Hancock, Typescript, BYU-S; http://www. boap.org/

PLACES

1. When was Nauvoo officially honored with the title, "The City of Joseph"?
   a. 1845, prior to the Saints' exodus to the West
   b. While Joseph Smith resided in Nauvoo and prior to his death in 1844
   c. At the time the Church purchased the temple lot
   d. At the time the Nauvoo Temple was dedicated by President Hinckley

2. What was Winter Quarters first called?
   a. Cutler Park
   b. Omaha
   c. Florence
   d. Little Nauvoo

3. Who did the Saints have to buy out to become the sole residents of Ray County, Missouri?
   a. Lilburn Boggs, since he owned the land
   b. Seven bee hunters
   c. The Native American tribe in the area
   d. The French, since the land was part of the Louisiana Purchase

4. Have you ever wondered how Temple Square ranks in places visited in the United States? Of the thousands of places to visit in this great country of ours, from National Parks to beaches to zoos to amusement parks to museums, you might be a little surprised at Temple Square's ranking. What's even more surprising are some of the places that Temple Square beats out. Which of the following options are two such places?
   a. Disneyland and Universal Studios
   b. Niagara Falls and Times Square
   c. Grand Canyon and Waikiki Beach
   d. The National Mall in Washington, DC, and the Las Vegas Strip

5. What was set up on the northeast corner of the temple block during part of the construction of the Salt Lake Temple?
   a. The stone cutters
   b. A temporary sawmill
   c. The tithing yard
   d. A molasses production site

6. Who dedicated the temple site at Manti, Utah?
   a. Moroni
   b. Brigham Young
   c. Wilford Woodruff
   d. Joseph Smith

7. In my book, *Unique Stories & Facts from LDS History*, I mention that Main Street in Salt Lake City, which was actually known as East Temple Street during pioneer times, was dubbed "Whiskey Street" because of all the saloons. What else was it known by?
   a. Perdition Street
   b. Hades Street
   c. Hell Street
   d. Devil Street

8. In 1842 a *Times and Seasons* article suggested that Lehi landed where in the new world?
   a. Chile
   b. Panama
   c. Mexico
   d. Guatemala

ANSWERS

1. a. 1845, prior to the Saints' exodus to the West

The following from the journal of Warren Foote dated April 7, 1845: "I took a severe cold yesterday and the wind blows very cold this morning, but I thought that I would attend conference which I did in the forenoon but I had to go to bed in the afternoon with a severe pain in my side. Brigham Young said today, 'From henceforth let this place [Nauvoo] be called the City of Joseph.' The congregation today was estimated at 20,000."

Autobiography of Warren Foote, Typescript, HBLL; http://www.boap. org/

2. a. Cutler Park

We then traveled on about half a day to a camping ground near a grove of timber which was called Cutler Park. The season now being so far spent and so many of our best young men gone to Mexico. President Young thought best to go no further this fall but find winter quarters cut hay for our stock and start on early in the spring. A town site was selected down the river called Winter Quarters. Streets, blocks and lots were layed out and given out to the people. And in a few days a town of houses were in sight. Lots of hay was cut and stock taken to herd grounds, a large log meeting house was built and a good grist mill was built to grind our corn and wheat. The people had brought with them houses and wood had to be provided for the families of the men that had gone in the battalion and there was a meat market erected and several blacksmith shops, shoe shops, chair makers and nearly all kind of work as if the people was going to stay for years.

Autobiography of Robert Gardner Jr., Typescript, HBLL; http://www. boap.org/

3. b. Seven bee hunters

William Edwin Berrett, The Restored Church *(Salt Lake City: Deseret Book, 1973), 131.*

4. c. Grand Canyon and Waikiki Beach

Here is the list detailing the average number of tourists per year.

1. Times Square, New York City: 37.6 million
2. Las Vegas Strip: 30 million
3. National Mall, Washington, DC: 25 million
4. Faneuil Hall, Boston: 20 million
5. Disney World: 17.1 million
6. Disneyland: 14.9 million
7. Fisherman's Wharf and Golden Gate Recreation Area, San Francisco: 14.1 million
8. Niagara Falls: 12 million
9. Great Smoky Mountains National Park: 9.04 million
10. Navy Pier, Chicago, Illinois: 8.6 million
11. Lake Mead National Recreation Area: 7.6 million
12. Universal Studios, Orlando, Florida: 6.2 million
13. SeaWorld, Florida: 5.8 million
14. Delaware Water Gap National Recreation Area, Philadelphia and New Jersey: 5.13 million
15. San Antonio River Walk: 5.1 million
16. Temple Square, Salt Lake City: 5 million
17. Universal Studios, Hollywood: 4.7 million
18. Metropolitan Museum, New York City: 4.7 million
19. Cape Cod National Seashore: 4.64 million
20. Grand Canyon: 4.43 million
21. Busch Gardens Africa, Tampa Bay: 4.4 million
22. SeaWorld, San Diego: 4.26 million
23. Independence National Historic Park, Philadelphia: 4.08 million
24. New York Museum of Natural History: 4 million
25. Waikiki Beach, Oahu, Hawaii: 3.67 million

Rob Baedeker, ForbesTraveler.com, February 20, 2009

5. d. A molasses production site

"The sugar beet equipment that the church purchased in 1852 was initially taken to Provo and then set up on the northeast corner of the temple block in Salt Lake City to make molasses. Eventually the equipment was moved four miles south of the city to the present-day location of what was eventually named Sugar House."

William Edwin Berrett, The Restored Church *(Salt Lake City: Deseret Book, 1973), 304.*

6. a. Moroni

The question is often asked, "How did the records that Mormon gave to Moroni about 385 AD and that the angel Moroni gave to Joseph Smith in 1827 AD get to the Hill Cumorah in New York? If the last battle was fought in Veracruz, Mexico, then Moroni must have carried the records to New York after the final battle at Ramah/Cumorah in Mesoamerica. The final battle was 385 AD; Moroni's last entry was 421 AD. That makes thirty-six years from the time of the last battle to Moroni's last dated entry. During the thirty-six years, he abridged the Jaredite record that we know as the Book of Ether; he finished the record of his father, Mormon; and he wrote material under his own name, which is the last book in the Book of Mormon.

Furthermore, he tells us that he did not make himself known to the Lamanites because they killed everyone who did not deny Christ; and he refused to deny Christ. After abridging the Book of Ether, Moroni very probably hid up, in the Mesoamerica Cumorah, the 24 gold plates from which he abridged the Jaredite record and then carried the abridged portion of the record to New York. He had ample time. His motivation to distance himself from the Lamanites is adequate.

One evidence of Moroni's wandering is a statement by Elder Franklin D. Richards of the Council of the Twelve. The incident he spoke of occurred at the temple-site dedication of the Manti Temple on April 25, 1877. Early that morning, Brigham Young had asked Warren S. Snow to go with him to the temple hill. According to Snow: "We two were alone; President Young took me to a spot where the temple was to stand; we went to the southeast corner, and President Young said: 'Here is the spot where the Prophet Moroni stood and dedicated this piece of land for a temple site, and that is the reason why the location is made here, and we can't move it from this spot.'"

Ensign, *January 1972, 33; Joseph L. Allen,* Exploring the Lands of the Book of Mormon *(Orem, Utah: S.A. Publishers, 1989), 351.*

The question still remains, would Moroni have been able to survive a trip of several thousand miles through strange peoples and lands, if he did transport the record?

Such a journey would be no more surprising than the trip by Lehi's party over land and by sea halfway around the globe. As a matter of fact, we do have a striking case of a trip much like the one Moroni may have made. In the mid-sixteenth century, David Ingram, a shipwrecked English sailor, walked in eleven months through completely strange Indian territory from Tampico, Mexico, to the St. John River, at the present border between Maine and Canada. His remarkable journey would have been about the same distance as Moroni's and over essentially the same route. So Moroni's getting the plates to New York even under his own power seems feasible.

"Man Alone," Christian Science Monitor *(June 1, 1967), 16; John L. Sorenson,* An Ancient American Setting For The Book of Mormon *(Salt Lake City: Deseret Book, 1985), 44–45.*

7. c. Hell Street

On Christmas day we had a scrap with the United States Soldiers. I saw in a certain history of Utah, that it was a row with a set of persons that were drunk. I ask in all reasons, why do people in getting up our histories resort to such abominable falsehoods? Why is it not as easy to tell the truth and shame satan as it is the wish of some to try to shame God and to raise satan to a standard? Have not our enemies been the petted and pampered ones long enough? And now I tell it. That command located in those barracks in Salt Lake City had been pampered by the elite of the city until they supposed that the majority of the women and the girls were their private property. Erma King was my partner as we were walking down the sidewalk on the East side of what was then know as Hell-Street, or Whiskey-Street. The walk was full of soldiers and some Mormons. Some of us were going to the Seventies Party at the Seventies Hall of Science. There came along two of the finest looking ladies I had ever beheld. There were two soldiers, or perhaps two sergeants, one of whom made such an expression right in front of the young ladies that all at once the blabbers head had broken a picket and his head lay between two more pickets. Then there was considerable stir. I saw that it was no place for my partner, so I hailed a team and having taken my partner in we stopped to see the rest of the play and I saw it all through. I had had no liquor of any kind. There might have been some under the influence of liquor to some extent, but if there were, I failed to see it on any one of them. We went on to our dance having an enjoyable time. Our dance being dignified, we closed at an early hour.

Autobiography of Mosiah Hancock, Typescript, BYU-S; http://www. boap.org/

8. b. Panama

What looks like the first consensual interpretation of Book of Mormon geography among him (Joseph Smith) and his associates was sweeping: The land southward was the whole of South America; the land northward, the North American continent. One indicator of that is an 1836 record in Frederick G. Williams's handwriting attributing the statement to Joseph Smith that "Lehi and his company . . . landed on the continent of South America, in Chile, thirty degrees, south latitude." Church leaders B. H. Roberts and John A. Widtsoe, both careful critics, were hesitant to accept the statements' origin with the Prophet, yet it certainly wouldn't be surprising if the Prophet had once held this view, since other early Church members seem to have believed it. [Williams later claimed that the statement about Chile was made to him by an angel rather than by Joseph.] In view of the fact that the Prophet's ideas matured on other subjects over time his thinking on Book of Mormon geography could also have undergone change. In 1842, an editorial in the Church newspaper the *Times and Seasons* [September 15, pages 921–22] asserted that "Lehi . . . landed a little south of the Isthmus of Darien [Panama]."

Compendium, *Franklin D. Richards and James A. Little, eds. (Salt Lake City: Deseret News Press, 1886), 289; Brigham H. Roberts,* New Witnesses for God, The Book of Mormon, *vol. 3 (Salt Lake City: Deseret News Press, 1926, 501–03; John A. Widtsoe, "Is the Book of Mormon Geography Known?" in* A Book of Mormon Treasury: Selections from the Pages of the Improvement Era *(Salt Lake City: Bookcraft, 1959), 128–29; Francis W. Kirkham,* A New Witness for Christ in America: The Book of Mormon *(Independence, MO: Zion's Printing and Publishing Co., 1942), 93.*

Scripture, Latter-day Saint Publications, and Writings

1. Abraham took Isaac to Mt. Moriah to sacrifice him. Where is Mt. Moriah?
   a. The location of Herod's Temple
   b. Bethlehem
   c. Golgotha
   d. Nazareth

2. Not only were the 116 pages lost by Martin Harris, but what other document went missing?
   a. The Lectures of Faith
   b. The revelation on the Word of Wisdom
   c. The history of the Church
   d. The original manuscript of the Book of Mormon

3. When Hyrum Smith brought installments every day of the Book of Mormon manuscript for John Gilbert to set the type, how did Hyrum bring it?
   a. In his hand in the open for all to see
   b. In a valise (small bag)
   c. Tucked up under his vest
   d. Rolled up in his top hat

4. What did Mrs. Harris (Martin Harris's wife) do at the Joseph Smith Sr. cabin near Palmyra, New York?
   a. Help Lucy Mack Smith milk the cow
   b. Heft the golden plates

   c.   Give Joseph Smith Jr. an earful for pulling Martin's attention away from their farm
   d.   Search for the plates when the Smiths weren't home

5.   The same press that printed the *Elder's Journal* in Far West, Missouri was used to print what publication in Nauvoo?
   a.   *The Nauvoo Neighbor*
   b.   *The Times and Seasons*
   c.   *The Wasp*
   d.   *The Nauvoo Expositor*

6.   The press that Sam Brannan used to print *The California Star* in Yerba Buena was used to print what other publication?
   a.   *The Wasp*
   b.   The Book of Mormon
   c.   *The Prophet*
   d.   *The Times and Seasons*

7.   True or false? We know what is contained in the sealed portion of the golden plates.

8.   The first edition of the Doctrine and Covenants included what?
   a.   Revelations only
   b.   Two articles by Oliver Cowdery
   c.   The Topical Guide
   d.   Faith-inspiring articles by Joseph Smith and his counselors

9.   Approximately how many gold leaves (plates) would have been needed to translate the 522 pages of the Book of Mormon?
   a.   45 pages
   b.   30 pages
   c.   60 pages
   d.   15 pages

10. The Popol Vuh is what?
   a.   Incan words for the Urim and Thummim
   b.   A papyrus found with the mummies that Joseph Smith purchased during the Kirtland years of the Church
   c.   A stella in the Andes of Peru, explaining the creation of the world
   d.   Ancient writing in the Quiche language of South America, closely akin to the stories found in the Bible

11. In today's Book of Mormon, the Testimony of the Three Witnesses is at the front. Where was it in the first edition?
    a. It was at the end of the book
    b. It was not included in the first edition
    c. It was at the front, like it is today
    d. It was in the Doctrine and Covenants

12. Who printed the first Church Almanac and in what year was it printed?
    a. John Taylor in 1844
    b. Parley P. Pratt in 1853
    c. The Kirtland Literary Firm in 1835
    d. Orson Pratt in 1845

13. What is the one book in the Book of Mormon that does not use the phrase, "And it came to pass?"
    a. Omni
    b. Moroni
    c. Words of Mormon
    d. Helaman

14. True or false? As a joke Martin Harris replaced the seerstone Joseph Smith was using with another stone.

15. When was the Bible first printed in America and where was it printed?
    a. 1777 in Philadelphia
    b. 1749 in Boston
    c. 1801 in Palmyra, New York
    d. 1761 in New York City

16. We believe the Bible as far as it is translated correctly. So the question may be asked, just how many times has the Bible been translated?
    a. 99 times
    b. 62 times
    c. 190 times
    d. 271 times

ANSWERS

1. a. The location of Herod's Temple

Abraham was commanded to sacrifice Isaac on Mt. Moriah. This is the same location of Herod's Temple in Jerusalem. Ironically another sacrifice, the sacrifice of our Savior, took place in the same area.

The Church of Jesus Christ of Latter-day Saints, Scripture Stories *(Salt Lake City: The Church of Jesus Christ of Latter-day Saints), 14.*

2. d. The original manuscript of the Book of Mormon

Not only were the 116 pages lost by Martin Harris, but the entire original manuscript was also lost. Hyrum Smith said that the manuscript, "once fell into the hands of an apostate (I [Hyrum] think one of the Whitmers) and they had to resort to stratagem to get possession of it again."

Letter from John Brown to John Taylor, December 20, 1879.

It is this manuscript that eventually found its way into the cornerstone of the Nauvoo House. Lewis Bidamon, second husband of Emma Smith, tore down the Nauvoo House and came across the box containing the original manuscript. Over time he gave portions of this manuscript away to a number of individuals, although it was in poor shape (placed in the Nauvoo House in 1841 and recovered in 1882).

Who were these people that received portions of this manuscript from Mr. Bidamon? One was Sarah M. Kimball. She received 1 Nephi 2:2 to 1 Nephi 13:35 on September 7, 1883.

> I asked the lady friend with whom I was riding to call with me on Mr. Bidamon a former acquaintance; after learning where I was from, he recognized me and seemed pleased, we talked a little of times that were, and of persons gone. . . . I referred to his home which is a temporary four room building on the southwest corner of the foundation laid for the Nauvoo House. I asked why the heavy and extensive foundations around him were being torn up, he replied, that he had bought the premises, and the rock was torn up to sell, as he was poor and otherwise would not have been able to build. I said, I am interested in this foundation, because I remember there were treasures deposited under the chief corner-stone. He said, yes, I took up the stone box and sold it . . . It had been so long exposed to the wet and weather that its contents were nearly ruined, I gave

the coin to Joe and told him he could have the pile of paper. He said it was the manuscript of the Book of Mormon; but it was so much injured that he did not care for it. While we were talking, Mr. Bidamon's wife brought a large pasteboard box and placed it on my lap. It contained a stack of faded and fast decaying paper, the bottom layers for several inches, were uniform in size, as they seemed to me larger than common foolscap, the paper was coarse in texture and had the appearance of having lain a long time in water, as the ink seemed almost entirely soaked into the paper, when I handled it, it would fall to pieces. I could only read a few words here and there just enough to learn that it was the language of the Book of Mormon. Above this were some sheets of finer texture folded and sewed together, this was better preserved and more easily read, I held it up, and said, "Mr. B. How much for this relic?" He said, "'Nothing from you, you are welcome to anything you like from the box." I appreciated the kindness, took the leaves that were folded and sewed together.

Letter from Sarah M. Kimball to George Reynolds, July 19, 1884.

Franklin D. Richards received 1 Nephi 15:5 to 2 Nephi 30 and Alma 2:19 to Alma 60:22 on May 21, 1885.

We were quite willingly shown all that remained of the Book of Mormon manuscript: . . . The paper is yellow with age and from the moisture sweated from its own hiding place. It is brittle to the touch. Many of the leaves crumble like ashes and some of them are broken away. It is necessary to handle them with the utmost care. The writing is faint, and is not legible on many continuous lines, but fragmentary clauses, and even whole verses are occasionally discernible. . . .

When the proprietor saw the profound interest with which we regarded these things, he spoke to us about them with great respect and generosity. We talked with him upon the subject of the writings at considerable length, and through his complaisance, when we came away we brought with us all of the manuscripts . . . and have them now in our possession.

Deseret News, *July 1, 1885, 380–81.*

Joseph W. Summerhays received one page, 1 Nephi 15:26–29, on October 3, 1884.

I was introduced to Major L.C. Bidamon. . . . I said to him Major they tell me over in Missouri that you have found the manuscript of the Book of Mormon in this house. How is it? He answered: In 1882 I

made some alterations in the house and in taking down the east wing in the southeast corner I came across a stone box about 10 x 15–6 inches deep. The box was sealed with a stone cap in it. I found a Bible, Book of Mormon, Doctrine and Covenants, Hymn Book, *Times and Seasons*, a letter addressed to the Pres. of the United States written by Lyman Wight, setting forth the wrongs of our people, some manuscript and less than one thousand dollars in cash (a joke), all in a bad state of preservation. Then turning to his wife he said to her, "bring the papers." Which she did. I examined them, especially the manuscript. I cannot tell what it is, for it is very rotten and the ink is faded but from the more visible, I make the following extracts: "And again I say unto to you that it is my will that my servant Lyman Wight should continue to preaching in Zion in the spirit of meekness confessing me before the world and I will bear him up as on Eagles wings and he shall beget glory and honor." I think this is from the Doc. and Cov. I quote further, "And they said unto me what meaneth the river of water which our father saw and I said unto them that the water which my father saw was filthiness and so much was his mind swallowed up in other things that he beheld not the filthiness of the water. I said unto them that it was an awful gulf which separated the wicked from the tree of life and also from the saints of God and I said unto them that it was a representation of that awful Hell which the Angel said unto me was prepared for the wicked." I think this is from the Book of Mormon. Some of the Manuscript was, I think, extracts from the Book of Mormon, and some from the Doc. and Cov. Some of it was in printer's takes and had been corrected. The pencil marks being plain and the ink faded. I asked the Major for some of the manuscript. He refused, but when he left the room his wife gave me one leaf and a few leaves of the Bible.
Diary of Joseph W. Summerhays, October 3, 1884.

Edward Stevenson stated that he received "a small portion as a relic, which I now have," in September of 1888.
Edward Stevenson, "Diary," September 12, 1888.

Andrew Jenson received a hat full of pieces that had broken off from the badly damaged manuscript on October 6, 1888.
Statement of Andrew Jenson, March 18, 1938.

Others having portions of the original manuscript are
A.B. Kesler of Salt Lake City
Deseret News, August 8, 1931

Community of Christ (Reorganized Church of Jesus Christ of Latter-day Saints)

Richard P. Howard, Restoration Scriptures: A Study of Their Textual Development *(Independence, MO: Herald Publishing House, 1969),* 27.

3. c. Tucked up under his vest

Hyrum carried the manuscript tucked up under his vest to hide it from the public. The following are recollections of John H. Gilbert, the typesetter for the Book of Mormon, many years after the fact.

> I am a practical printer by trade. I have been a resident of Palmyra, New York, since about the year 1824, and during all that time have done some typesetting each year. I was aged ninety years on the 13th day of April 1892, and on that day I went to the office of the Palmyra Courier and set a stickful of type.
>
> My recollection of past events, and especially of the matters connected with the printing of the "Mormon Bible" [Book of Mormon], is very accurate and faithful, and I have made the following memorandum at request, to accompany the photographs of "Mormon Hill," which have been made for the purpose of exhibits at the World's Fair in 1893.
>
> In the forepart of June, 1829, Mr. E. B. Grandin, the printer of the *Wayne Sentinel,* came to me and said he wanted I should assist him in estimating the cost of printing 5,000 copies of a book that Martin Harris wanted to get printed, which was called the "Mormon Bible." It was the second application of Harris to Grandin to do the job—Harris assuring Grandin that the book would be printed in Rochester if he declined the job again.
>
> Harris proposed to have Grandin do the job, if he would, as it would be quite expensive to keep a man in Rochester during the printing of the book, who would have to visit Palmyra two or three times a week for manuscript, etc. Mr. Grandin consented to do the job if his terms were accepted.
>
> A few pages of the manuscript were submitted as a specimen of the whole, and it was said there would be about 500 pages.
>
> The size of the page was agreed upon, and an estimate of the number of ems in a page, which would be 1,000, and that a page of manuscript would make more than a page of printed matter, which proved to be correct.
>
> The contract was to print, and bind with leather, 5,000 copies

for $3,000. Mr. Grandin got a new font of small pica, on which the body of the work was printed.

When the printer was ready to commence work, [Martin] Harris was notified, and Hyrum Smith brought the first installment of manuscript, of 24 pages, closely written on common foolscap paper—he had it under his vest, and vest and coat closely buttoned over it. At night [Hyrum] Smith came and got the manuscript, and with the same precaution carried it away. The next morning with the same watchfulness, he brought it again, and at night took it away. This was kept up for several days. The title page was first set up, and after proof was read and corrected, several copies were printed for Harris and his friends. On the second day—[Martin] Harris and [Hyrum] Smith being in the office—I called their attention to a grammatical error, and asked whether I should correct it? [Martin] Harris consulted with [Hyrum] Smith a short time, and turned to me and said, "The Old Testament is ungrammatical, set it as it is written."

After working a few days, I said to [Hyrum] Smith on his handing me the manuscript in the morning, "Mr. [Hyrum] Smith, if you would leave this manuscript with me, I would take it home with me at night and read and punctuate it, and I could get along faster in the daytime, for now I have frequently to stop and read half a page to find how to punctuate it." His reply was, "We are commanded not to leave it." A few mornings after this, when [Hyrum] Smith handed me the manuscript, he said to me, "If you will give your word that this manuscript shall be returned to us when you get through with it, I will leave it with you." I assured Smith that it should be returned all right when I got through with it. For two or three nights I took it home with me and read it, and punctuated it with a lead pencil. This will account for the punctuation marks in pencil, which is referred to in the Mormon Report, an extract from which will be found below.

Martin Harris, Hyrum Smith and Oliver Cowdery, were very frequent visitors to the office during the printing of the Mormon Bible [Book of Mormon]. The manuscript was supposed to be in the handwriting of [Oliver] Cowdery. Every chapter, if I remember correctly, was one solid paragraph, without a punctuation mark, from beginning to end.

Names of persons and places were generally capitalized, but sentences had no end. The character or short "&" was used almost invariably where the word "and" occurred, except at the end of a chapter. I punctuated it to make it read as I supposed the author intended, and but very little punctuation was altered in proofreading.

The Bible [Book of Mormon] was printed sixteen pages at a time, so that one sheet of paper made two copies of sixteen pages each, requiring 2,000 sheets of paper for each form of sixteen pages. There were thirty-seven forms of sixteen pages each—570 pages in all.

The work was commenced in August 1829 and finished in March 1830—seven months. Mr. J. H. Bortles and myself did the presswork until December taking nearly three days to each form.

In December Mr. Grandin hired a journeyman pressman, Thomas McAuley, or "Whistling Tom," as he was called in the office, and he and Bortles did the balance of the presswork. The Bible [Book of Mormon] was printed on a "Smith" Press, single pull, and old-fashioned "Balls" or "Niggerheads" were used—composition rollers not having come into use in small printing offices.

The printing was done in the third story of the west end of "Exchange Row," and the binding by Mr. Howard, in the second story; the lower story being used as a bookstore, by Mr. Grandin, and now—1892—by Mr. M. Story as a dry goods store.

[Oliver] Cowdery held and looked over the manuscript when most of the proofs were read. Martin Harris once or twice, and Hyrum Smith once, Grandin supposing these men could read their own writing as well, if not better, than anyone else; and if there are any discrepancies between the Palmyra edition and the manuscript these men should be held responsible.

Joseph Smith, Jr., had nothing to do whatever with the printing or furnishing copy for the printers, being but once in the office during the printing of the Bible [Book of Mormon], and then not over fifteen or twenty minutes.

Hyrum Smith was a common laborer, and worked for anyone as he was called on.

[Oliver] Cowdery taught school winters—so it was said—but what he did summers, I do not know.

Martin Harris was a farmer, owning a good farm, of about 150 acres, about a mile north of Palmyra Village, and had money at interest. Martin—as everybody called him—was considered by his neighbors a very honest man; but on the subject of Mormonism, he was said to be crazy. Martin was the main spoke in the wheel of Mormonism in its start in Palmyra, and I may say, the only spoke. In the fall of 1827, he told us what wonderful discoveries Jo [Joseph] Smith had made, and of his finding plates in a hill in the town of Manchester (three miles south of Palmyra),—also found with the plates a large pair of "spectacles," by putting which on his nose and looking at the plates, the spectacles turned the hieroglyphics into good English. The question might be asked here whether Jo [Joseph] or the spectacles was the translator?

Sometime in 1828, Martin Harris, who had been furnished by someone with what he said was a facsimile of the hieroglyphics of one of the plates started for New York. On his way he stopped at Albany and called on Lieutenant Governor Bradish—with what success I do not know. He proceeded to New York, and called on Professor C. Anthon, made known his business and presented his hieroglyphics.

This is what the professor said in regard to them—1834—

The paper in question was, in fact, a singular scroll.

It consisted of all kinds of singular characters, disposed in columns, and had evidently been prepared by some person who had before him, at the time, a book containing various alphabets; Greek and Hebrew letters, crosses and flourishes, Roman letters inverted or placed sidewise, arranged and placed in perpendicular columns, and the whole ended in a rude delineation of a circle, divided into various compartments, arched with various strange marks, and evidently copied after the Mexican Calendar, given by Humboldt, but copied in such a way as not to betray the source whence it was derived. I am thus particular as to the contents of the paper, inasmuch as I have frequently conversed with my friends on the subject since the Mormon excitement began, and well remember that the paper contained anything else but "Egyptian Hieroglyphics."

Martin [Harris] returned from this trip east satisfied that "Joseph" was a "little smarter than Professor Anthon."

Martin was something of a prophet—he frequently said that "Jackson would be the last president that we would have; and that all persons who did not embrace Mormonism in two years' time would be stricken off the face of the earth." He said that Palmyra was to be the New Jerusalem, and that her streets were to be paved with gold.

Martin was in the office when I finished setting up the testimony of the Three Witnesses—([Martin] Harris, [Oliver] Cowdery and [David] Whitmer). I said to him, "Martin, did you see those plates with your naked eyes?" Martin looked down for an instant, raised his eyes up, and said, "No, I saw them with a spiritual eye."

Recollections of John H. Gilbert [Regarding printing the Book of Mormon], 8 September 1892, Palmyra, New York, Typescript, BYU; http://www.boap.org/

4. b. Heft the golden plates
The following from Martin Harris:

I then thought of the words of Christ, The kingdom divided against itself cannot stand. I knew they were of the devil's kingdom, and if that is of the devil, his kingdom is divided against itself. I said in my heart, this is something besides smoke. There is some fire at the bottom of it. I then determined to go and see Joseph as soon as I could find time. A day or so before I was ready to visit Joseph, his mother came over to our house and wished to talk with me. I told her I had no time to spare, she might talk with my wife, and, in the evening when I had finished my work I would talk with her. When she commenced talking with me, she told me respecting his bringing home the plates, and many other things, and said that Joseph had sent her over and wished me to come and see him. I told her that I had a time appointed when I would go, and that when the time came I should then go, but I did not tell her when it was. I sent my boy to harness my horse and take her home. She wished my wife and daughter to go with her; and they went and spent most of the day. When they came home, I questioned them about them. My daughter said, they were about as much as she could lift. They were now in the glass-box, and my wife said they were very heavy. They both lifted them. I waited a day or two, when I got up in the morning, took my breakfast, and told my folks I was going to the village, but went directly to old Mr. Smith's.

"Mormonism—II," Tiffany's Monthly 5 (August 1859): 163–70. Copy located at American Antiquarian Society, Worcester, Massachusetts.

5. b. The *Times and Seasons*

In each of the locations the Saints had gathered, a printing press and a Church publication had been started. So in Nauvoo one of the first achievements was the establishment of a printing press. On the night that the mob forces of General Lucas had surrounded Far West, the Church printing press, used at that place for the publication of the *Elders Journal*, was hidden from the enemy and buried in the dooryard of a Brother Dawson. Later it was secretly dug up and shipped to Commerce, Illinois. There it was set up again in a cellar during the fall of 1839. On this press was published the fourth periodical of the Church, the *Times and Seasons*.

William Edwin Berrett, The Restored Church (Salt Lake City: Deseret Book, 1973), 162.

6. c. *The Prophet*

"In January, 1847, [Samuel] Brannan began the publication of the Yerba Buena *California Star*, using the press on which *The Prophet* had been printed by the Saints in New York. This was the first newspaper printed in San Francisco and the second English paper in California."

William Edwin Berrett, The Restored Church *(Salt Lake City: Deseret Book, 1973), 231.*

7. True

On one of Joseph's visits with the angel Moroni, the angel told Joseph: "The sealed part contains the same revelation which was given to John upon the isle of Patmos, and when the people of the Lord are prepared, and found worthy, then it will be unfolded unto them."

Milton V. Backman Jr. and Keith W. Perkins, Writings of Early Latter-day Saints and Their Contemporaries—Database. Provo, Utah: Religious Studies Center, 1996.

8. b. Two articles by Oliver Cowdery

"Two articles written by Oliver Cowdery on Marriage and Governments in General."

Teachings of the Prophet Joseph Smith, *Joseph Fielding Smith, comp. (Salt Lake City: Deseret Book, 1976), 8.*

9. a. 45 pages

"It is estimated that less than forty-five plates, engraved on both sides, would be necessary for the entire record translated, including that portion for which the translation was lost."

J.M. Sjodahl, An Introduction to the Study of the Book of Mormon *(Salt Lake City: Deseret News Press, 1927), 42.*

10. d. Ancient writing in the Quiche language of South America, closely akin to the stories found in the Bible

> The most authentic source book for these legends is the Popol Vuh, a rare manuscript written in the Quiche language and translated into the Spanish by Francisco Jimenez, a well-known Catholic priest who lived among the Indians of Guatemala during the early Spanish rule of America. This interesting volume is replete with stories so closely akin to those of the Hebrews that one noted scholar, Le Plongeon, declared that these stories originated in America and were later carried to the old world where the Hebrews adopted and

improved upon them. Le Plongeon claimed to have found upon the walls of old buildings at Chichen-Itza and Uxmal, in Central America, mural paintings of the creation, the temptation of Eve in the garden of Eden, the story of Cain and Abel, and many others of the Hebrew legends.

William Edwin Berrett, The Restored Church *(Salt Lake City: Deseret Book, 1973), 64.*

11. a. It was at the end of the book

Note where in the Book of Mormon John Corrill reads the testimony of the Three witnesses: "In the course of two or three days, the book of Mormon, (the Golden Bible, as the people then termed it, on account of its having been translated from the Golden plates,) was presented to me for perusal. I looked at it, examined the testimony of the witnesses at the last end of it, read promiscuously a few pages, and made up my mind that it was published for speculation."

John Corrill, A Brief History of the Church of Christ of Latter-Day Saints (Commonly Called Mormons, Including an Account of their Doctrine and Discipline, with the Reasons of the Author for Leaving the Church) *(St. Louis, n.p., 1839).*

12. d. Orson Pratt in 1845

Although the Literary Firm in Kirtland, Ohio, had planned to issue an almanac in the 1830s, the first one actually published by a Latter-day Saint was Orson Pratt's *Prophetic Almanac for 1845.* It borrowed heavily from the standard American almanacs of the day, with a calendar and astronomical data along with the birth and death dates of secular leaders and prominent individuals. Elder Pratt also included some of his own doctrinal teachings, as well as those of his brother Parley and of Joseph Smith.

Orson Pratt's second effort, the *Prophetic Almanac for 1846,* was more distinctly Mormon with its exclusion of secular names and dates and the inclusion of dates of Latter-day Saint interest. In this issue he continued his missionary vent with doctrinal pieces and information. His intention was to publish the almanac annually, but these were the only two. He prepared one for 1849 at Winter Quarters, but there was no way to publish it.

W. W. Phelps published the *Deseret Almanac* between 1851 and 1866 in Salt Lake City. From 1859 to 1864 it was called *The Almanac.* The fourteen issues again borrowed from standard almanacs of the day, with the inclusion of religious and cultural articles uniquely pertaining to Latter-day Saints. He also included items of medical, agricultural, and social information.

David J. Whittaker, "Almanacs in the New England Heritage of Mormonism." BYU Studies *4 (Fall 1989), 89–113; Arnold K. Garr, Donald Q. Cannon, and Richard O. Cowan,* Encyclopedia of Latter-day Saint History *(Salt Lake City: Deseret Book, 2000), 19–20.*

13. b. Moroni

The phrase "and it came to pass" occurs in the English translation of the Book of Mormon 1,381 times. It appears 202 times in 1 Nephi alone. The Book of Alma records the highest number of "it came to pass" phrases: 431. Only the Book of Moroni fails to use the phrase "and it came to pass."

The phrase "and it came to pass" is not unique to the Book of Mormon, as the Bible utilizes the same introductory phrase. "And it came to pass," or one of its derivatives, occurs 526 times in the Old Testament and 87 times in the New Testament. This fact suggests that the phrase "and it came to pass" is Hebrew in origin and correlates with Nephi's statement.

Apparently the Maya people, who lived in Southeast Mexico and Guatemala, may have adopted the phrase "and it came to pass." Recent discoveries in the translations of the glyphs of the seven century AD Maya ruins of Palenque manifest the phrase "and then it came to pass" and "it had come to pass." Recently, another glyph has been interpreted as "and it shall come to pass."

Joseph L. Allen, Exploring the Lands of the Book of Mormon *(Orem, Utah: S.A. Publishers, 1989), 31–32.*

14. True

He also stated that the Prophet translated a portion of the Book of Mormon with a seerstone in his possession. The stone was placed in a hat that was used for that purpose, and with the aid of this seerstone the Prophet would read sentence by sentence as Martin wrote, and if he made any mistake the sentence would remain before the Prophet until corrected, when another sentence would appear. When they became weary, as it was confining work to translate from the plates of gold, they would go down to the river and throw stones into the water for exercise. Martin on one occasion picked up a stone resembling the one with which they were translating, and on resuming their work,

Martin placed the false stone in the hat. He said that the Prophet looked quietly for a long time, when he raised his head and said: "Martin, what on earth is the matter, all is dark as Egypt." Martin smiled and the seer discovered that the wrong stone was placed in the hat. When he asked Martin why he had done so he replied, to stop the mouths of fools who had declared that the Prophet knew by heart all that he told him to write, and did not see by the seerstone; when the true stone was placed in the hat, the translation was resumed, as usual.

Edward Stevenson, "The Three Witnesses to the Book of Mormon," Millennial Star *48 (21 Jun 1886), 389–91.*

15. a. 1777 in Philadelphia
David Daniell, The Bible in English: Its History and Influence *(New Haven and London: Yale University Press, 2003)*

16. c. 190 times
David Daniell, The Bible in English: Its History and Influence *(New Haven and London: Yale University Press, 2003)*

ABOUT THE AUTHOR

Dan Barker was born in Montana and raised in Calgary, Alberta, Canada. He served in the Massachusetts Boston Mission and has enjoyed Church callings in the Primary, Sunday School, and elders quorum. He currently serves as an instructor in his high priests group and as the ward emergency specialist.

He has an associates diploma from Lethridge Community College with a major in wildland park management and a bachelor of science degree from Utah State University with a major in forestry. Dan enjoyed an abbreviated career with the forest service and is now currently employed with Nestle.

Dan and Kate Nelson married in the Cardston Alberta Temple thirty years ago and have six children and eleven grandchildren. They currently live in Orem, Utah.

He is the author of *Leaders, Managers, and Blue Collar Perceptions* and *Unique Stories & Facts from LDS History*. Dan welcomes reader feedback. You may contact him via email at danbarker@dbnkids.com.

0 26575 57984 0